How We Became Human

New and Selected Poems

ALSO BY JOY HARJO

An American Sunrise
Conflict Resolution for Holy Beings
Crazy Brave: A Memoir
Soul Talk, Song Language: Conversations with Joy Harjo
For a Girl Becoming
A Map to the Next World
The Good Luck Cat
The Spiral of Memory
The Woman Who Fell from the Sky
Fishing
In Mad Love and War
Secrets from the Center of the World
The Woman Hanging from the Thirteenth Floor Window
New Orleans
She Had Some Horses
Remember
What Moon Drove Me to This?
The Last Song

EDITED BY JOY HARJO

Reinventing the Enemy's Language:
Contemporary Native Women's Writings of North America

MUSIC ALBUMS

Red Dreams, a Trail Beyond Tears
Winding Through the Milky Way
She Had Some Horses
Native Joy for Real
Letter from the End of the Twentieth Century

PLAYS

Wings of Night Sky, Wings of Morning Light

How We Became Human

New and Selected Poems

JOY HARJO

W. W. Norton & Company   New York   London

Credits:
Poems from *The Last Song,* originally published by Puerto Del Sol Press, from
New Mexico State University, copyright © Joy Harjo 1975. Reprinted by per-
mission of the author. Poems from *What Moon Drove Me to This?,* copyright ©
Joy Harjo 1980, reprinted by permission of the author. Poems from *She Had
Some Horses* by Joy Harjo, copyright © 1983, 1997 by Thunder's Mouth
Press, appear by their permission. Poetic prose from *Secrets from the Center of
the World* by Joy Harjo and Stephen Strom, copyright © 1989 The Arizona
Board of Regents, are reprinted by permission of the Arizona University Press.
Poems from *In Mad Love and War,* copyright © 1990 by Joy Harjo, are reprinted
by permission of Wesleyan University Press. Poems from *Arabian Love Poems*,
by Nizar Kabbani, translated by Bassam K. Frangish and Clementine R.
Brown, English text of poems copyright © 1993 by Bassam K. Frangish and
Clementine R. Brown. Reprinted with permission of Lynne Rienner Publishers,
Inc. Excerpt from "Lucille" by Kenny Rogers is reprinted by permission of
SBK Entertainment World. Poems from *The Woman Who Fell from the Sky,*
copyright © 1994, and *A Map to the Next World,* copyright © 2000, are
reprinted by permission of W. W. Norton.

The text of this book is composed in DeVinne with the display set in Torino
Composition by Tom Ernst
Manufacturing by LSC Harrisonburg
Book design by Dana Sloan
Production manager: Julia Druskin

Library of Congress Cataloging-in-Publication Data

Harjo, Joy.
    How we became human : new and selected poems / Joy Harjo.—1st ed.
        p. cm.
Includes index.
    ISBN 0-393-05101-3
    1. Indians of North America—Poetry. 2. Navajo Indians—Poetry. 3.
Indian women—Poetry. I. Title.
    PS3558.A62423 H69 2002
    811'.54—dc21

                                                                2002000871

ISBN 978-0-393-32534-8 pbk.

W. W. Norton & Company, Inc., 500 Fifth Avenue, New York, N.Y. 10110
www.wwnorton.com

W. W. Norton & Company Ltd., 15 Carlisle Street, London W1D 3BS

    5 6 7 8 9 0

For my sisters and brothers, by blood and by love

For my allies, and for my enemies

For my heart

What kind of nation is this
Deleting love from its curriculum
The art of poetry
The mystery of women's eyes
What kind of nation is this
Battling each rain cloud . . .

—Nizzar Kabbani

✖ CONTENTS

from *In Mad Love and War*, 1990, Wesleyan University Press

from *The Woman Who Fell from the Sky*, 1994, W. W. Norton

from *A Map to the Next World: Poems and Tales,* 2000, W. W. Norton

New Poems, 1999–2001

ACKNOWLEDGMENTS

This work has been supported through the years by so many and so much it is not possible to name everyone. You know who you are, and many of you may not know who you are—this includes all who have ferried me to and from airports, have cooked and cleaned and carried the trash, for all those who continue to read, think, and dream in poetry.

And for those who have supported the poetry by nurturing it, by publishing it, the list is long and includes: Puerto del Sol Press from New Mexico State University; Ishmael Reed and Steve Cannon of their imprint I. Reed Books, a press that started many of us on our careers; Neil Ortenberg and crew at Thunder's Mouth Press, now part of Avalon; Larry Evers and Ofelia Zepeda and everyone else at the University of Arizona Press; Wesleyan University Press (and Tom Radko there), who continues to publish fine poetry; Ox Head Press; Jill Bialosky, who has faithfully birthed my books of poetry into the world, and W. W. Norton, who continues to give important attention to poetry; and Laura Coltelli, a soulmate of poetry who has translated several of these books into Italian and has given them a place in her most beloved country. *Grazie. Mvto.* Thank you.

And for all those who helped with the compilation and research for notes, including Maggi Michel, Rainy Ortiz, George Coser Jr., Simon Ortiz, Lurline McGregor, Carmen Foghorn, Karen and Stephen Strom, Patsy Mae Jojola, Laura Coltelli, Carolyn Dunn, Tim Chee, Sue Williams, Nadema Agard, Craig Womack, Father John Staudenmaier, and Pam

Uschuk and Bill Root, who helped me find the title as well as gave advice with notes while Mars slowly circled.

My family is huge and grows each journey I make into the world. There would be no poetry without them. This includes my sister Margaret Ann Barrows, who inspires her students at Liberty Mounds School to write poetry. She has always been by my side through the terrible tests of childhood, through the making of poetry. And my sister Sandy Aston, who gave me love when there appeared to be little. And welcome, our newly found sister Debbie. And my brothers Allen and Boyd Foster. I do poetry and music. They do cars and trucks. And Greg Sarris, for your love, your stories. And Debra Haaland, your chile and kindnesses sustain me. I thank you Phil for your humor, and belief in me, and Rainy for your compassionate vision, your love and Ratonia for your bravery. And the two new souls who have joined us on this road of poetry: my grandsons Tayo and Chayson; my cousins George Coser Jr. and Pete Coser; and my family at the Tvlvhasse Ceremonial Grounds including Sam and David Proctor, Craig, Gerardo, Joyce and all the rest.

I cannot forget the gifts from the Indian school years, from the jazzers in Denver, from Simon Ortiz, June Jordan, Audre Lorde, Diane Reyna, Rosalyn Drexler, Rain Parrish, Pat Jojola, Ron Rogers, Geary Hobson, Quincy Troupe, Larry Emerson, Ali Darwish and Cairo and my relatives there; from this beloved island of O'ahu and the Hawaiian people here; for Lesline Conner, for Keone Nunes, for Bill and Mary Tiger. Thank you Barbara and all the HT family. And all the horses, especially Casey—here's a thank-you in horse language.

And to all elements that make petit dejeuner in Paris and in Papeete, Tahiti, with Wailana, possible. *Mvto*. For Lurline Wailana McGregor, you know how I mean. *Mahalo*. To the Pacific, the earth and sky. And to all the other family who have inspired me as I searched for poetry. *Mvto*. For my mother, who is at the center of this journey. And my father. I thank you for this life, this breath. *Mvto*. May I return it with *vnokeckv* (love).

INTRODUCTION

It was around the time we lost Larry Casuse to the racist guns of the Gallup police. He and Robert Nakaidinae emerged from the mayor's office, where they had been holding the mayor hostage for crimes against Indian people. They came out with their hands up. The police shot to kill anyway. This wasn't anything new, but now the hatred had come out into the open. It was erupting.

I was losing it, my car kept trying to drive itself off the road, and at any moment I would shatter. I was a broke Indian student with small children, immersed in painting and drawing classes at the University of New Mexico, trying to make it through a relationship with someone with whom I felt a powerful kinship, but who, too, was caught in the undertow of a few centuries of this country's denial. He responded by drinking with such a vigor as if to kill himself and then the anger would overflow. He would either disappear to rage or sing or tell stories that overwhelmed with their intense velocity, or he would attempt to tear down the house. My response was to turn inward with the snap of the wave, and I shivered to a breakdown, to an earthquake of the heart. I could not swallow without great difficulty, and had to calculate each step forward, literally so it was quite a feat to get the stroller loaded with books, paints, diapers, and lunchpails and make it the three blocks to the university and day care.

Sometimes I joined in the revelry in the bars or after hours and drank to obliterate the pain. A memory bleeds through of a bar on the main street of downtown, before downtown had been gentrified. Above the door was a sign that always cracked us up: THROUGH THESE DOORS WALK SOME OF THE FINEST PEOPLE IN THE WORLD. The memory is smokey, as is the bar and we seem like ghosts as we dance to the jukebox or play pool or fight. In my memory I am whirling in a sea of dancers in cowboy hats and long black hair. I feel like a ghost as I return to this memory, returning in a different body, in a different time. There's a crash of glass as a pitcher slams against the wall, barely missing some-one's head. The two men struggle and in their wake is a path of broken chairs, tossed barstools, old girlfriends, and uncried tears. A pool of blood looks black in mercury lighting and I can't remember anything.

Otherwise I kept painting, and after I had cooked dinner, given the children their baths, and put them to bed I was free to roam in the disap-pearance zone, into the realm of creativity, idea, and follow design, curve, and meaning out of the disturbance and the world of sharp edges, to sense and beauty. This place was familiar to me. When I was three or four I took chalk and made the slate-walled garage into a mural. I took crayons and decorated the closet in the bedroom shared by my two broth-ers and sister. Always my art took place in private places, in the dark, far from public view. Even then, it was what I wanted to do with my life, "to be an artist," I always answered.

In the Mvskoke world women are accepted as painters, artists. To make art (whether it be painting, drawing, songs, stories—any art) is to replicate the purpose of original creation. My favorite aunt Lois Harjo Ball was a painter, as was my grandmother Naomi Harjo Foster. I grew up with my grandmother's art on the walls of our home, until our father left and took all of it with him when he fled after the divorce. He took all except for a charcoal of two horses running in a storm, a copy she had done of a popular image of her time. Lois kept up her painting through the years, though painted less the few years before her death in a nursing home in Okmulgee. My grandmother died when my father was young but left quite a few paintings. Many of their paintings are in the collection of the Creek Council House Museum.

During that time of becoming a painter I went into Langell's art store to buy supplies and canvas. In the aisle for oil paints I recognized Pablita Velarde, the well-known Pueblo painter who was also shopping for supplies. She smiled at me and said hello, gave a recognition of me as a fellow Indian woman artist. That brief encounter gave me a shot of courage that lasted for days. I shone and I kept going.

At the pinnacle of the breakdown I was in the student union at lunchtime with some of my Kiva Club friends. They dragged me over to an older Indian woman who was psychic; they told me she helped the police find missing people. I was curious, and somewhat reluctant. No one knew that I was near suicide, no one knew that even as we were speaking with each other I was counting steps and giving my body instructions on how to move so that I would not whirl and fall apart. I cannot. I cannot, I told myself in a small internal voice, because I have children who are relying on me and there would be no one there if it all fell apart. She opened my palm then quickly closed it. She saw it all, and I saw her see it all. She told me to be careful, to take care of myself.

Here is where poetry showed up, at this intersection of a glimmer of self-knowledge and the need to make art of whatever materials are at hand. Poetry approached me in that chaos of raw inverted power and leaned over and tapped me on the shoulder, said, "You need to learn how to listen, you need grace, you need to learn how to speak. You're coming with me." I did not walk off into the sunset with poetry, or hit the town with a blaze of gunfire with poetry guarding my back. Rather, the journey toward poetry worked exactly as the process of writing a poem. It started from the inside out, then turned back in to complete a movement. And then on and on in the manner of a ripple in water, a song in the air.

This was the first poetry, the raw questioning, the falling-in-love-with-poetry poetry, the open-your-eyes-and-ears poetry, the first-legs-of-a-newborn-creature poetry. It started here, with a glimmer, a thought, the need to speak, with an impulse fed by history, dream, myth (that is, myth as an archetypal reality, not as falsehood), belief, and most of all faith. This poetry made roots from the compelling need to speak, to hear, to walk gracefully from one century to the next—despite the lines at the food stamp office, changing diapers, writing papers for classes, organizing for political action—without the luxury of a wife, a washer and dryer, a cook or nanny or a known library of publications by Indian writers. These were the early poems of the chapbook, *The Last Song*, sewn together at a table at David Apodaca's kitchen in Las Cruces, New Mexico, and the book that followed from Ishmael Reed and Steve Cannon's press, I. Reed Books, *What Moon Drove Me to This?* It was a poetry that could not have been written without the mentoring of Simon Ortiz, an Acoma poet—who when he told me he was an Indian poet, probably at some meeting at the National Indian Youth Council where he worked with Gerry Wilkinson, I wanted to ask, What is that? but I didn't dare. His poetry was the opening. It was shortly after that time I met the Laguna Pueblo poet and writer Leslie Silko, who came home to New Mexico for a visit, to get out of the rain of Ketchikan, Alaska, where she was writing her first novel, *Ceremony*. Her poetry and stories inspired me, gave form and sensibility to my early writing. And then Scott Momaday, the Kiowa writer who was awarded the Pulitzer Prize for his groundbreaking novel, *House Made of Dawn*, who came to speak at the University of Iowa where I was a graduate student—his writing and speaking taught me lessons in eloquence, dignity. And James Welch, the Blackfeet poet and writer who made me laugh despite the terrible lessons of being Indian in this country, and then the Oneida poet Roberta Hill, whose complex, tough, and beautiful poetry led me to the poet Richard Hugo—his poetry taught me that becoming human was the most honorable task of poetry.

It was in 1979 when I was teaching at the Institute of American Indian Arts in Santa Fe and in the middle of writing the poems of what would become *She Had Some Horses,* that I squeezed as many creative writing students as I could into my small Japan-made truck and we headed to Albuquerque to spend the day with Richard Hugo, who was giving a writing workshop and a reading at the University of New Mexico. Though Hugo was already a legend to me, I didn't expect his luminosity, the shine of his compassion. He was generous with my students and they were moved by his reading that night to a packed house. That language has color, weight, breath and garnered as much presence as a painting, jewelry, or any other of their arts—that poetry is a river of history moving through the blood tree of the body was his gift to them that night. I can still see them lined up along the back row of the auditorium, listening to Hugo's poems and the poignant and witty stories that accompanied his poems. As we gathered up to leave someone asked, "Where's Yazzie?"* "She's at Okie's," someone answered. So, I drove to Okie's first, to retrieve Yazzie, a brilliant young Navajo woman majoring in pottery, who was there but not there. Half of her soul was enmeshed in the internal battle of what am I in this place of loss and heartbreak? How do I bear the weight of my soul?

The struggle was private, disturbing. We were always concerned about her. Would she make it? And what does "make it" mean in the whole scheme of the world? Perhaps "not making it" in one world was food for making it in another. When her spirit broke free she was tattered, raw, and beautiful.

That night, then, became a Richard Hugo poem: a truck of Indian students headed to Okie Joe's bar to retrieve a lost beloved one in a land that had been taken from us—a land no one could own. I sent a student in to find Yazzie. He didn't return. I then sent the next volunteer, then

* Not her real name.

the next until I was the only one left, and had to go into that place to bring everyone home. Everyone came, but Yazzie. We couldn't find her. She eventually found herself, but not that night, not for many nights.

And in those earlier years there were many poets: Leo Romero, the poet from Chacon who fostered my journey toward poetry, when I doubted it. He successfully made the leap back and forth between drawing and writing. Ishmael Reed and his multicultural gatherings, including my first visit to New York City in the late seventies where I heard Jayne Cortez perform, and gained sustenance from the various poets in that gathering: from Puerto Rican to Irish to Filipino to Chicano to Jewish to African-American, a gathering of inclusion. Not long after I was invited to the One World Poetry Festival in Amsterdam and I realized there were many poetries from all over the world, just as there were, I was learning, poetry in all of the native tribes of North America, over five hundred viable tribal groups. Poetry was not under the ownership or province of Europe or New England, though it often appeared otherwise. Something was born in that realization, given life. It was like the shock of first learning the earth was not flat as many generations before you had assumed, but round. Or now that the world is neither flat nor round but in the shape of a spiral, the shape of the mind of God.

There were many poets whose poetry sustained me in those times, and continue to sustain me: Pablo Neruda, June Jordan, Amos Tutuola, Jean Toomer, Ricardo Sanchez, Judy Grahn, Galway Kinnell, Audre Lorde, William Butler Yeats, Lawson Inada, García Lorca, Anne Sexton, Sylvia Plath, Okot p'Bitek. They are part of an overlapping circle.

Until then, writing poetry had not been an option, especially as a career, an occupation, a journey for life. Riding bulls was a possibility, being a car mechanic or sheet-metal worker like my father, a tribal chief like my grandfather, a cook and waitress like my mother or even a painter, like my aunt and grandmother. Becoming a wife and mother was primary, a career was something that happened at divorce for my mother's relatives who were poor. My grandmother and aunt had the option to be artists because oil was discovered on their allotted lands. They had options that weren't available for my mother. Until then, becoming a poet was no longer the sole territory of white people from the northeast United States or Europe.

All this is the context of . . . Horses, what the horses mean, a kind of love, brought together despite an opposition of culture, of place and time.

The poet cannot be separated from place. Even placelessness becomes a place. The world of conjecture, scholarship, and philosophical discourse is a place or series of places, based on land and how one lives off that land. The collaboration with the astronomer and photographer Stephen Strom, *Secrets from the Center of the World*, is a tribute to a land, a people, to particular stars and heavenly bodies who are part of that land, the history, myth, and shape of it. I believe Strom's study of the birth of stars has much to do with his photographic vision; there's a depth measured by light-years rather than miles, in the tender rendering of his photographs.

My journey on this earth in this life is marked by a path of red earth that leads from the mounds at Ocmulgee in what is now known as Georgia, to The Battle of Horsehoe Bend site at a curve in the Talapoosa River in now-Alabama, to the Mvskoke Creek Nation in now-Oklahoma, to the grounds of Indian school in now-New Mexico, and since that collection has taken me to the red earth of O'ahu. It makes a distinct path. It is the color of blood, it is the color of a collection of stars, it is the color of life, of breath. And, as anything in life that is a vital part of us, it needs to be fed with songs, poems; it needs to be remembered, hence, this collection of poetic prose and photographs.

This earth asks for so little from us human beings.

It was a fall day in Tempe. This meant a particular smell on the breeze, the Sun heading to a more northern elliptic. The children had gone to school and I sat outside facing east, with a terrible restlessness. I was in the presence of the Sun, a higher being than us small humans, and I was in the presence of the being higher than that, and I was in my human body that was flooded with passion and longing. I was being asked a question, and I have an innate aversion to being asked questions.

We had an argument, or more exactly, a discussion, for those higher ones do not argue. There is no need. I was ultimately arguing with myself. Would I continue toward enlightenment or would I veer off? I was at that proverbial crossroads. Every day is a crossroads, what we eat, what we think, what we do decides the direction, the path, but some crossroads yield greater consequences. I was reminded of a similar time, another fall day several years before. I was in the backseat of a car, driving from an afternoon of several pitchers of beer at the bar. I remember the smell of damp leaves and the gray sky, the light mist of a rain. I had been out the night before, and the night before that and was aware that the high of forgetfulness was seducing me, and I liked the seduction, the sense of flight when after a few drinks I could do anything, be anyone I wanted, and the pain went away. The pain, however, didn't go far. It was always there when I awoke from the illusion, a pounding in my head, my heart, a bag of guilt larger than the sky. I remember the laughter of the woman driving us, a laugh crusty with smoke and tears. I was aware that there was a choice. I could go either way. I asked her to drive me home. In that moment my heart suddenly grew large with compassion for her, for all of us, and I realized that later, knowing this would be crucial information, something I needed to know.

That morning in the early eighties in that small patch of desert I temporarily called home, I said I wasn't ready. I wanted to test the limits of passion, I wanted to do what I wanted to do. I wanted my childhood back, like a two-year-old, by myself. Thus began my *mad love and war.* Of course, I didn't understand the consequences of my choice until seven years later, when I made a conscious turn back, when I looked out over the wreckage and saw the gleam of hard-won knowledge. This has everything to do with poetry, which is the making of songs for ceremonial or secular use. It's all sacred. Every wrong turn is eventually a right turn.

It was the poetry of jazz during the mid-eighties that gave me the saxophone so I could sing my way through the mess, as had Billie Holiday, John Coltrane, Charlie Parker, Jim Pepper, and all the rest of the mostly unknown. Night after night I immersed myself in the language of jazz as interpreted by the jazzers of Denver: Ron Henry, Billy Wallace, Laura Newman, and all the rest, at either El Chapultepec or any of the other clubs that have come and gone. The language of jazz kept me up at night or woke me up early in the morning as I wrote in the manner of the horn riffs that carried me over the battlefield:

The opposite of love is not hate. It is disinterest, distraction. Where can my baby be? Hate attracts hate and the blues are the consequence of blues. If love attracts love, then where can my baby be?

I had to sing it and for the first time I needed a saxophone so that poems would have accompaniment for the songs of love and war. The horn could laugh, could cry in a direct, physical manner. Poetry and music belonged together. This was not new as poetry and music have been together since the invention of poetry and music. They are soul mates, not meant to be parted. It is only in the modern age they were separated: when the printing press was invented, when the self-appointed keepers of the sacred pronounced the body was not the house of the spirit. Most of the world's literature is still oral, not written.

There are still many ongoing wars. For my nation and many other tribal nations these wars are still being fought, only the battlefield these days is most often in the courts. During the eighties I made trips to Nicaragua, to the border of El Salvador, and to Honduras as part of goodwill missions and poetry festivals. I saw guns on a table of negotiations and on the shoulders of young men and women barely out of childhood. In Miskito country the people were not on either side, like our people up north they, too, did not believe in ownership of land, the selling of souls. In them I saw my own people in an early era of colonization and I knew I had to go home. I turned back and was forced to face the source of the war:

The opposite of love is not love. It is fear. Where can my nation be?
Hate attracts hate and the blues are the consequence of blues. If fear
destroys love, then where can my nation be?

And around that time, in the twilight between the last round and dawn, the bass player began having dreams. Every night as she closed her eyes to dream they would appear in her room. Sometimes there was only one Aboriginal man from Australia, or there would be several gathered there in her room in her rented house in Denver. They would stand there, as if she were calling them. She didn't know what to do, she told us. She knew they weren't of evil intent but she was disturbed at their inconceivable presence. She was walking around in a no-sleep daze. Then one afternoon she was leafing through a coffee-table book on the Aboriginal people and saw it, the stone, a stone she had picked up somewhere on her hikes in the mountains of Colorado. It looked exactly like the dreaming stone in the photograph. "What did you do with it?" we asked her. "I took it to the mountains and threw it in the water," she said. And the Aboriginals quit showing up and then she could sleep.

There is no separation between poetry, the stories and events that link them, or the music that holds all together, just as there is no separation between human, animal, plant, sky, and earth. When The Woman Who Fell from the Sky landed, she landed on a turtle who graciously offered his back. When she landed she planted the seeds that she carried in her hands. She planted herself and consequently all who would come after her. This was the beginning of the North American continent, according to the Iroquois.

In 1990 I attended the Continental Meeting of Indigenous People in Quito, near where clouds are born. Indigenous peoples from the whole hemisphere, all the way from the North Pole to Tierra del Fuego had gathered for an historic meeting, to tell the stories of our nations since the arrival of Christopher Columbus—whom the rest of the world was preparing to celebrate—to share ideas, strategies, and always food and music. I had come down with Patti Blanco to pass out flyers and talk to women for a proposed anthology of native women's writing, Reinventing the Enemy's Language, which originally was going to include indigenous women of the whole hemisphere. In one of the women's meetings a striking Bolivian Indian woman stood up to welcome the group:

"I'd like to welcome all of you to this place we have come together, from many nations, many countries. . . . I'd especially like to welcome those of you from the United States of America. We thought John Wayne had killed all of you."

Everyone laughed, but she was serious. Movies are how most of the world knows anything about America or American culture(s).

"And I'd like to ask you why you call only yourselves America? This land is one body, we are one people. We are all America."

And with that we set to work to discuss policy, issues, solutions and to add our work to the larger resolution being assembled by all in attendance.

My poems from this era are of an awareness of being part of a continuum in which there is no separation of form or being: one people is related to another, this world is related to the next, that is: death is not the opposite of life. A story leads to a dream leads to a poem leads to a song and so on.

Audre Lorde's death in the early nineties marked the transformation of a warrior in this world, a poet-warrior who worked for justice for women, for lesbians, for black women and ultimately all. The poet in the role of warrior is an ancient one. The poet's road is a journey for truth, for justice. One is not liberated if another is enslaved. Compassion is the first quality of a warrior, and compassion is why we are here, why we fell from the sky. The kitchen table is the turtle's back on which this work is accomplished.

I always wished for a map to show the way. When we come into this world, from the other side of death, we mark our existence with a cry. My granddaughter Krista came in with her eyes wide open, with a shout. I fought and struggled and nearly killed both my mother and me. "Where is the map?" I asked. I want to see the map, first. The church people told me it was the Bible. The historians said, look back and then you can move forward. The ceremonial songs sing that it is all around you. The poets tell me it is in the heart, where poetry is born and the place it enters when it is finished. This is all true.

Several years later and I am at that familiar crossroads again. I have just finished a performance on a stage with my band Poetic Justice, within feet and a few hours of an explosion of a bomb that will kill visitors, and will shut down the Olympics for a few days. We are at the epicenter. The whole world is shaken. I know that I cannot continue living the way I have been living, in a house that is not my house, in a country in which I have become a stranger. That night behind the hotel several miles from the center of Atlanta we stomp-danced. I did not stop.

All of these poems are an offering to the source of poetry. We must feed the spirit of poetry, of song making just as we feed our bodies to give them energy, or feed our minds with thoughts. It is important to offer a little tobacco or something of what we are eating, so that the spirit of poetry is acknowledged, welcomed, and returns again with new insight, as a companion into the territory of an art made of philosophy, vision, blood, and music.

What amazed me at the beginning and still amazes me about the creative process is that even as we are dying something always wants to be born.

SEPTEMBER 2001

From
The Last Song

WATCHING CROW, LOOKING SOUTH TOWARD THE MANZANO MOUNTAINS

crow floats in winter sun
a black sliver
in a white ocean of sky
crow is the horizon
drifting south of Albuquerque

the horizon dances
along the blue edge
of the Manzanos
wind is an arch
a curve
on the black wing of crow

a warm south wind
if it stays for a while
will keep a crow dancing for thirty years
on the ridge
of a blue mountain breeze

FOR A HOPI SILVERSMITH

he has gathered the windstrength
from third mesa
into his hands
and cast it into silver

i have wanted to see
the motion of wind
for a long time

thank you
for showing me

SAN JUAN PUEBLO AND SOUTH DAKOTA ARE
800 MILES AWAY ON A MAP

for Barbara Wells-Faucon

who does he think he is
he's just a Sioux anyway
she said
drinking a little faster
to catch up

behind her hand
we laugh
because we know how Siouxs are
and we know that we are drunk

words are scattered quickly
into the loud jukebox
    music
my voice recedes far away
into the mouth of the Sandias

but she is dancing
at Pine Ridge
inside his wild horse eyes

HE TOLD ME HIS NAME WAS SITTING BULL

the great-grandson of the old chief
and he reached across my arm
to fill his glass
from the pitcher
that is his excuse to sit closer

"where you from"
    he is from southwest oklahoma
    i am from the northeast part

"i have been looking for you for six
hundred miles," he tells me
and the grassy plains near anadarko
he spreads out for me
in the brown hills of his eyes
    i smile   hiding my teeth
between the branches of oaks
in tahlequah hills

"come with me" he squeezes my arm
the sioux horseman rides away across
                        my shoulder
i shake my head
and drown his horse in the water
of the illinois river

the young warrior drops his hand
but he never surrenders
his name
      will follow me on the interstate
all the way into the center of oklahoma

3 A.M.

in the Albuquerque airport
trying to find a flight
to Old Oraibi, Third Mesa
TWA
    is the only desk open
bright lights outline New York
              Chicago
and the attendant doesn't know
that Third Mesa
is a part of the center
of the world
and who are we
just two indians
at three in the morning
trying to find a way back

and then I remembered
that time Simon
took a Yellow Cab
out to Acoma from Albuquerque
a twenty-five dollar ride
to the center of himself

3 A.M. is not too late
to find the way back

THE LAST SONG

how can you stand it
he said
the hot oklahoma summers
where you were born
this humid thick air
is choking me
and i want to go back
to new mexico

it is the only way
i know how to breathe
an ancient chant
that my mother knew
came out of a history
woven from wet tall grass
in her womb
and i know no other way
than to surround my voice
with the summer songs of crickets
in this moist south night air

oklahoma will be the last song
i'll ever sing

ARE YOU STILL THERE?

there are sixty-five miles
of telephone wire
between acoma
      and albuquerque
i dial the number
and listen for the sound
of his low voice
      on the other side
hello
   is a gentle motion of a western wind
cradling tiny purple flowers
that grow near the road
        toward laguna
i smell them
as i near the rio puerco bridge
my voice stumbles
returning over sandstone
     as it passes the canoncito exit
i have missed you he says
the rhythm circles the curve
of mesita cliffs
    to meet me
but my voice is caught
shredded on a barbed wire fence
at the side of the road
and flutters soundless
in the wind

CONVERSATIONS BETWEEN HERE AND HOME

Emma Lee's husband beat her up
this weekend,
his government check was held up
and he borrowed the money
to drink on.
Anna had to miss one week of work
because her youngest child
got sick
she says, "It's hard sometime, but
easier than with a man."
"I haven't seen Jim for two weeks
now," his wife tells me on the phone.
(I saw him Saturday with that Anadarko
woman.)

Angry women are building
houses of stones.
They are grinding the mortar
between straw-thin teeth
and broken families.

From
What Moon
Drove
Me to This?

FOUR HORSE SONGS

1. White One

the white horse
from the north clouds
sings from a dakota night
it is a pint of cheap vodka
that keeps him warm
as he dances
two feet off the ground
swaying from bar to bar
drinking his way south
he is the desperate one
who laughs too loud
at his own fate

2. Red One

the red horse
from the eastern sunrise
cannot see the next day
as he chases his life
across the streets of Gallup
he knows only
his red shameful eyes
in the morning
and it becomes
the same day always

3. Gray One

    this horse stayed south
    too near the railroad tracks
    his bones are gray
    in the dry sunlight
    he wanted to go home
    but the tracks always led
    to the same place

4. Yellow One

    yellow horse
    gallops home near Tsaile
    the sun is low and almost gone
    but he has faith
    in its returning

I AM A DANGEROUS WOMAN

The sharp ridges of clear blue windows
motion to me
from the airport's second floor.
Edges dance in the foothills of the Sandias
behind security guards
who wave me into their guncatcher machine.

I am a dangerous woman.

When the machine buzzes they say
to take off my belt,
and I remove it so easy
that it catches the glance
of a man standing nearby.
(Maybe that is the deadly weapon
that has the machine singing.)

I am a dangerous woman,

but the weapon is not visible.
Security will never find it.
They can't hear the clicking
of the gun inside my head.

THERE WAS A DANCE, SWEETHEART

It was a dance,
her back against the wall
at Carmen's party. He was alone
and he called to her—come here, come here.
That was the first time she saw him
and she and Carmen later drove him home
and all the way he talked to the moon
to stars and to someone riding
in the backseat that she
and Carmen didn't hear.

And the next time was either a story
in one of his poems, or what
she had heard from crows
gathered before snow caught
in the wheels of traffic silent
up and down Central Avenue.
He was two thousand years old.
She ran the bars with him
before the motion of snow
caught her, too, and he moved in.
It was dance.

In the dance were mesas winding
off the western horizon, the peak
of Mount Taylor that burned up

every evening at dusk light.
And in rhythm were mountain curves
that she fell against every night looking up
looking up. She knew him then, or maybe
it had been the motion of crows
against the white cold and power lines.
The voice that was him moved in her,
rocked in her and then the child
small and dark in the dance
dance dance of the dance.

There was no last time she saw him.
He returned with stars, a certain moon
and in other voices like last night.
She heard him first. Screen door slammed
against the wall. Crows outside
the iced tight windows.
Which dance, locked and echoed and sucked
the cliffs of her belly in?
She picked up their baby from the crib,
more blankets to tuck them in.
Loud he called—come here, come here.

It was a dance.

CROSSING THE BORDER

We looked the part.
It was past midnight, well into
the weekend. Coming out of Detroit
into the Canada side, border guards
and checks. We are asked, "Who are you Indians
and which side are you from?"
Barney answers in a broken English.
He talks this way to white people
not to us. "Our kids."
My children are wrapped
and sleeping in the backseat.
He points with his lips to half-eyed
Richard in the front.
"That one, too."
But Richard looks like he belongs
to no one, just sits there wild-haired
like a Menominee would.
"And my wife. . . . " Not true.
But hidden under the windshield
at the edge of this country
we feel immediately suspicious.
These questions and we don't look
like we belong to either side.

"Any liquor or firearms?"
He should have asked that years ago

and we can't help but laugh.
Kids stir around in the backseat
but it is the border guard who is anxious.
He is looking for crimes, stray horses
for which he has no apparent evidence.

"Where are you going?"
Indians in an Indian car, trying
to find a Delaware powwow
that was barely mentioned in Milwaukee.
Northern singing in the northern sky.
Moon in a colder air.
Not sure of the place but knowing the name
we ask, "Moravian Town?"

The border guard thinks he might have
the evidence. It pleases him.
Past midnight.
Stars out clear into Canada
and he knows only to ask,
"Is it a bar?"

Crossing the border into Canada,
we are silent. Lights and businesses
we drive toward could be America, too,
following us into the north.

SOMEONE TALKING

They watch the glittering moon
from the front porch in the middle of Iowa.
Which reservation
is this river of star motion?
The Man of Words sits next to
Noni Daylight
listening this time.

       Tequila, a little wine
       and she remembers some whiskey
       yellow in a fifth on the drainboard.
       She thinks of him
       in Oklahoma, how he drank with her
       the summer powwow in Anadarko.
       Where is the word for a warm night
       and how it continues to here
       a thousand miles from that time?
Milky Way.
And there are other words
in other languages, always
in movement. He touches
her back where her hair
reaches to the middle. There
is that gesture and the
cricket's voice beginning
all in the same circle of space.

Maybe the Man of Words speaks
like the cricket.
Noni Daylight
hears him
that way.

> It is along the Turner Turnpike
> between Tulsa and Oklahoma City,
> she tells him
> where they have all those signs:
> Kickapoo, Creek, Sac and Fox
> dating the beginning and end
> of the United States' recognition
> of tribal histories.
> And hell,
> Where is he now
> when she needs and tastes
> the crazy whiskey
> yellow fire all the way
> into her belly.
> The way they meant it.

They have maps
named after Africa and the blue oceans.
Sky circles the other way
but she doesn't feel dizzy.
Stars in the dark are clear,
not blurred, and the earth's movement
is a whirring current in the grass.

The Man of Words outlines wet islands
with his lips
on Noni Daylight's neck.
> She got stopped outside
> of Anadarko once.
> Red lights
> And you must be Indian, said
> the Oklahoma Highway Patrol.
> Of course, they knew the history
> Before switching on the lights.
> And when they rolled open the truck
> in the moist night
> she was only going home,
> she said.
What voice
in the warm grass of her belly?
What planet?

FIRE

a woman can't survive
by her own breath
        alone
she must know
the voices of mountains
she must recognize
the foreverness of blue sky
she must flow
with the elusive
bodies
of night winds
who will take her
into herself

look at me
i am not a separate woman
i am the continuance
of blue sky
i am the throat
of the mountains
a night wind
who burns
with every breath
she takes

From

She Had
Some Horses

CALL IT FEAR

There is this edge where shadows
and bones of some of us walk
backwards.
Talk backwards. There is this edge.
Call it an ocean of fear of the dark. Or
name it with other songs. Under our ribs
our hearts are bloody stars. Shine on
shine on, and horses in their galloping flight
strike the curve of ribs.

Heartbeat
and breathe back
sharply. Breathe
backwards.
There is this edge
within me

I saw it once
an August Sunday morning
when the heat hadn't
left this earth. And Goodluck
sat sleeping next to me in the
truck.
We had never broken through
the edge of the
singing at four A.M.

We had only wanted to talk, to hear
any other voice to stay alive with—

And there was this edge
not the drop of sandy rock cliff
bones of volcanic earth into

Albuquerque.
Not that,
but a string of shadow
horses kicking
and pulling me out of my
belly,
not into the Rio Grande
but into the music
barely coming through

Sunday church singing
from the radio. Battery worn-
down but the voices
talking backwards.

ANCHORAGE

for Audre Lorde

This city is made of stone, of blood, and fish.
There are Chugatch Mountains to the east
and whale and seal to the west.
It hasn't always been this way, because glaciers
who are ice ghosts create oceans, carve earth
and shape this city here, by the sound.
They swim backwards in time.

Once a storm of boiling earth cracked open
the streets, threw open the town.
It's quiet now, but underneath the concrete
is the cooking earth,
                and above that, air
which is another ocean, where spirits we can't see
are dancing   joking   getting full
on roasted caribou, and the praying
goes on, extends out.

Nora and I go walking down 4th Avenue
and know it is all happening.
On a park bench we see someone's Athabascan
grandmother, folded up, smelling like 200 years
of blood and piss, her eyes closed against some
unimagined darkness, where she is buried
in an ache in which nothing makes sense.

We keep on breathing, walking, but softer now,
the clouds whirling in the air above us.
What can we say that would make us understand
better than we do already?
Except to speak of her home and claim her
as our own history, and know that our dreams
don't end here, two blocks away from the ocean
where our hearts still batter away at the muddy shore.

And I think of the 6th Avenue jail, of mostly native
and black men, where Henry told about being shot at
eight times outside a liquor store in L.A., but when
the car sped away he was surprised he was alive,
no bullet holes, man, and eight cartridges strewn
on the sidewalk all around him.

Everyone laughed at the impossibility of it,
but also the truth. Because who would believe
the fantastic and terrible story of all of our survival
those who were never meant
                                        to survive?

FOR ALVA BENSON, AND FOR THOSE WHO HAVE LEARNED TO SPEAK

And the ground spoke when she was born.
Her mother heard it. In Navajo she answered
as she squatted down against the earth
to give birth. It was now when it happened,
now giving birth to itself again and again
between the legs of women.

Or maybe it was the Indian Hospital
in Gallup. The ground still spoke beneath
mortar and concrete. She strained against the
metal stirrups, and they tied her hands down
because she still spoke with them when they
muffled her screams. But her body went on
talking and the child was born into their
hands, and the child learned to speak
both voices.

She grew up talking in Navajo, in English
and watched the earth around her shift and change
with the people in the towns and in the cities
learning not to hear the ground as it spun around
beneath them. She learned to speak for the ground,
the voice coming through her like roots that
have long hungered for water. Her own daughter
was born, like she had been, in either place

or all places, so she could leave, leap
into the sound she had always heard,
a voice like water, like the gods weaving
against sundown in a scarlet light.

The child now hears names in her sleep.
They change into other names, and into others.
It is the ground murmuring, and Mount Saint Helens
erupts as the harmonic motion of a child turning
inside her mother's belly waiting to be born
to begin another time.

And we go on, keep giving birth and watch
ourselves die, over and over.
And the ground spinning beneath us
goes on talking.

THE WOMAN HANGING FROM
THE THIRTEENTH FLOOR WINDOW

She is the woman hanging from the 13th floor
window. Her hands are pressed white against the
concrete moulding of the tenement building. She
hangs from the 13th floor window in east Chicago,
with a swirl of birds over her head. They could
be a halo, or a storm of glass waiting to crush her.

She thinks she will be set free.

The woman hanging from the 13th floor window
on the east side of Chicago is not alone.
She is a woman of children, of the baby, Carlos
and of Margaret, and of Jimmy who is the oldest.
She is her mother's daughter and her father's son.
She is several pieces between the two husbands
she has had. She is all the women of the apartment
building who stand watching her, watching themselves.

When she was young she ate wild rice on scraped down
plates in warm wood rooms. It was in the farther
north and she was the baby then. They rocked her.

She sees Lake Michigan lapping at the shores of
herself. It is a dizzy hole of water and the rich
live in tall glass houses at the edge of it. In some

places Lake Michigan speaks softly, here, it just sputters
and butts itself against the asphalt. She sees
other buildings just like hers. She sees other
women hanging from many-floored windows
counting their lives in the palms of their hands
and in the palms of their children's hands.

She is the woman hanging from the 13th floor window
on the Indian side of town. Her belly is soft from
her children's births, her worn Levi's swing down below
her waist, and then her feet, and then her heart.
She is dangling.

The woman hanging from the 13th floor hears voices.
They come to her in the night when the lights have gone
dim. Sometimes they are little cats mewing and scratching
at the door, sometimes they are her grandmother's voice,
and sometimes they are gigantic men of light whispering
to her to get up, to get up, to get up. That's when she wants
to have another child to hold onto in the night, to be able
to fall back into dreams.

And the woman hanging from the 13th floor window
hears other voices. Some of them scream out from below
for her to jump, they would push her over. Others cry softly
from the sidewalks, pull their children up like flowers and gather
them into their arms. They would help her, like themselves.

But she is the woman hanging from the 13th floor window,
and she knows she is hanging by her own fingers, her
own skin, her own thread of indecision.

She thinks of Carlos, of Margaret, of Jimmy.
She thinks of her father, and of her mother
She thinks of all the women she has been, of all
the men. She thinks of the color of her skin, and
of Chicago streets, and of waterfalls and pines.
She thinks of moonlight nights, and of cool spring storms.
Her mind chatters like neon and northside bars.
She thinks of the 4 A.M. lonelinesses that have folded
her up like death, discordant, without logical and
beautiful conclusion. Her teeth break off at the edges.
She would speak.

The woman hangs from the 13th floor crying for
the lost beauty of her own life. She sees the
sun falling west over the gray plane of Chicago.
She thinks she remembers listening to her own life
break loose, as she falls from the 13th floor
window on the east side of Chicago, or as she
climbs back up to claim herself again.

WHITE BEAR

She begins to board the flight
    to Albuquerque. Late night.
But stops in the corrugated tunnel,
    a space between leaving and staying,
where the night sky catches

        her whole life

she has felt like a woman
    balancing on a wooden nickel heart
approaching herself from here to
    there, Tulsa or New York
with knives or cornmeal.

The last flight someone talked
    about how coming from Seattle
the pilot flew a circle
    over Mount Saint Helens; she sat
quiet (but had seen the eruption
    as the earth beginning
to come apart, as in birth
    out of violence).

She watches the yellow lights
    of towns below the airplane flicker,
fade and fall backwards. Somewhere,

she dreamed, there is the white bear
moving down from the north, motioning her paws
      like a long arctic night, that kind
of circle and the whole world balanced in
      between carved of ebony and ice

            oh so hard

the clear black nights
      like her daughter's eyes, and the white
bear moon, cupped like an ivory rocking
      cradle, tipping back it could go
either way
                  all darkness

                        is open to all light.

SKELETON OF WINTER

These winter days
I've remained silent
as a white man's watch
keeping time
         an old bone
empty as a fish skeleton
at low tide.
It is almost too dark
         for vision
these ebony mornings
but there is still memory,
the other-sight
and still I see.

Rabbits get torn under
cars that travel at night
but come out the other
side, not bruised
breathing soft
like no fear.

And sound is light, is
movement. The sun revolves
and sings.

There are still ancient
symbols

alive
I did dance with the prehistoric horse
years and births later
near a cave wall
late winter.

A tooth-hard rocking
in my belly comes back,
something echoes
all forgotten dreams,
        in winter.

I am memory alive
        not just a name
but an intricate part
of this web of motion,
meaning: earth, sky, stars circling
my heart

        centrifugal.

REMEMBER

Remember the sky you were born under,
know each of the star's stories.
Remember the moon, know who she is.
Remember the sun's birth at dawn, that is the
strongest point of time. Remember sundown
and the giving away to night.
Remember your birth, how your mother struggled
to give you form and breath. You are evidence of
her life, and her mother's, and hers.
Remember your father. He is your life, also.
Remember the earth whose skin you are:
red earth, black earth, yellow earth, white earth
brown earth, we are earth.
Remember the plants, trees, animal life who all have their
tribes, their families, their histories, too. Talk to them,
listen to them. They are alive poems.
Remember the wind. Remember her voice. She knows the
origin of this universe.
Remember you are all people and all people
are you.
Remember you are this universe and this
universe is you.
Remember all is in motion, is growing, is you.
Remember language comes from this.
Remember the dance language is, that life is.
Remember.

NEW ORLEANS

This is the south. I look for evidence
of other Creeks, for remnants of voices,
or for tobacco brown bones to come wandering
down Conti Street, Royal, or Decatur.
Near the French Market I see a blue horse
caught frozen in stone in the middle of
a square. Brought in by the Spanish on
an endless ocean voyage he became mad
and crazy. They caught him in blue
rock, said
  don't talk.

I know it wasn't just a horse
     that went crazy.

Nearby is a shop with ivory and knives.
There are red rocks. The man behind the
counter has no idea that he is inside
magic stones. He should find out before
they destroy him. These things
have memory,
  you know.

I have a memory.
     It swims deep in blood,

a delta in the skin. It swims out of Oklahoma,
deep the Mississippi River. It carries my
feet to these places: the French Quarter,
stale rooms, the sun behind thick and moist
clouds, and I hear boats hauling themselves up
and down the river.

My spirit comes here to drink.
My spirit comes here to drink.
Blood is the undercurrent.

There are voices buried in the Mississippi mud.
There are ancestors and future children
buried beneath the currents stirred up by
pleasure boats going up and down.
There are stories here made of memory.

I remember DeSoto. He is buried somewhere in
this river, his bones sunk like the golden
treasure he traveled half the earth to find,
came looking for gold cities, for shining streets
of beaten gold to dance on with silk ladies.

He should have stayed home.

       (Creeks knew of him for miles
       before he came into town.

Dreamed of silver blades
and crosses.)

And knew he was one of the ones who yearned
for something his heart wasn't big enough
to handle.
          (And DeSoto thought it was gold.)

The Creeks lived in earth towns,
          not gold,
   spun children, not gold.
That's not what DeSoto thought he wanted to see.
The Creeks knew it, and drowned him in
    the Mississippi River
          so he wouldn't have to drown himself.

Maybe his body is what I am looking for
as evidence. To know in another way
that my memory is alive.
But he must have got away, somehow,
because I have seen New Orleans,
the lace and silk buildings,
trolley cars on beaten silver paths,
graves that rise up out of soft earth in the rain,
shops that sell black mammy dolls
holding white babies.

And I know I have seen De Soto,
        having a drink on Bourbon Street,
        mad and crazy
        dancing with a woman as gold
        as the river bottom.

SHE HAD SOME HORSES

She had some horses.

She had horses who were bodies of sand.
She had horses who were maps drawn of blood.
She had horses who were skins of ocean water.
She had horses who were the blue air of sky.
She had horses who were fur and teeth.
She had horses who were clay and would break.
She had horses who were splintered red cliff.

She had some horses.

She had horses with eyes of trains.
She had horses with full, brown thighs.
She had horses who laughed too much.
She had horses who threw rocks at glass houses.
She had horses who licked razor blades.

She had some horses.

She had horses who danced in their mothers' arms.
She had horses who thought they were the sun and their
bodies shone and burned like stars.
She had horses who waltzed nightly on the moon.
She had horses who were much too shy, and kept quiet
in stalls of their own making.

She had some horses.

She had horses who liked Creek Stomp Dance songs.
She had horses who cried in their beer.
She had horses who spit at male queens who made
them afraid of themselves.
She had horses who said they weren't afraid.
She had horses who lied.
She had horses who told the truth, who were stripped
bare of their tongues.

She had some horses.

She had horses who called themselves, *horse*.
She had horses who called themselves, *spirit,* and kept
their voices secret and to themselves.
She had horses who had no names.
She had horses who had books of names.

She had some horses.

She had horses who whispered in the dark, who were afraid
to speak.
She had horses who screamed out of fear of the silence, who
carried knives to protect themselves from ghosts.
She had horses who waited for destruction.
She had horses who waited for resurrection.

She had some horses.

She had horses who got down on their knees for any saviour.
She had horses who thought their high price had saved them.
She had horses who tried to save her, who climbed in her
bed at night and prayed as they raped her.

She had some horses.

She had some horses she loved.
She had some horses she hated.

These were the same horses.

I GIVE YOU BACK

I release you, my beautiful and terrible
fear. I release you. You were my beloved
and hated twin, but now, I don't know you
as myself. I release you with all the
pain I would know at the death of
my children.

You are not my blood anymore.

I give you back to the soldiers
who burned down my home, beheaded my children,
raped and sodomized my brothers and sisters.
I give you back to those who stole the
food from our plates when we were starving.

I release you, fear, because you hold
these scenes in front of me and I was born
with eyes that can never close.

I release you
I release you
I release you
I release you

I am not afraid to be angry.
I am not afraid to rejoice.

I am not afraid to be black.
I am not afraid to be white.
I am not afraid to be hungry.
I am not afraid to be full.
I am not afraid to be hated.
I am not afraid to be loved.

to be loved, to be loved, fear.

Oh, you have choked me, but I gave you the leash.
You have gutted me but I gave you the knife.
You have devoured me, but I laid myself across the fire.

I take myself back, fear.
You are not my shadow any longer.
I won't hold you in my hands.
You can't live in my eyes, my ears, my voice
my belly, or in my heart my heart
my heart my heart

But come here, fear
I am alive and you are so afraid
                              of dying.

From

Secrets from
the Center
of the World

MY HOUSE IS THE RED EARTH

My house is the red earth; it could be the center of the world. I've heard New York, Paris, or Tokyo called the center of the world, but I say it is magnificently humble. You could drive by and miss it. Radio waves can obscure it. Words cannot construct it, for there are some sounds left to sacred wordless form. For instance, that fool crow, picking through trash near the corral, understands the center of the world as greasy scraps of fat. Just ask him. He doesn't have to say that the earth has turned scarlet through fierce belief, after centuries of heartbreak and laughter—he perches on the blue bowl of the sky, and laughs.

IF YOU LOOK WITH THE MIND OF
THE SWIRLING EARTH

If you look with the mind of the swirling earth near Shiprock
you become the land, beautiful. And understand how three
crows at the edge of the highway, laughing, become three crows
at the edge of the world, laughing.

IF ALL EVENTS ARE RELATED

for Wailana

If all events are related, then what story does a volcano erupting in Hawai'i, the birth of a woman's second son near Gallup, and this shoulderbone of earth made of a mythic monster's anger construct? Nearby a meteor crashes. Someone invents aerodynamics, makes wings. The answer is like rushing wind: simple faith.

THIS LAND IS A POEM

This land is a poem of ochre and burnt sand I could never write, unless paper were the sacrament of sky, and ink the broken line of wild horses staggering the horizon several miles away. Even then, does anything written ever matter to the earth, wind, and sky?

ANYTHING THAT MATTERS

Anything that matters is here. Anything that will continue to matter in the next several thousand years will continue to be here. Approaching in the distance is the child you were some years ago. See her laughing as she chases a white butterfly.

INVISIBLE FISH

Invisible fish swim this ghost ocean now described by waves of sand, by water-worn rock. Soon the fish will learn to walk. Then humans will come ashore and paint dreams on the drying stone. Then later, much later, the ocean floor will be punctuated by pickup trucks, carrying the dreamers' descendents, who are going to the store.

DON'T BOTHER THE EARTH SPIRIT

Don't bother the earth spirit who lives here. She is working on a story. It is the oldest story in the world and it is delicate, changing. If she sees you watching she will invite you in for coffee, give you warm bread, and you will be obligated to stay and listen. But this is no ordinary story. You will have to endure earthquakes, lightning, the deaths of all those you love, the most blinding beauty. It's a story so compelling you may never want to leave; this is how she traps you. See that stone finger over there? That is the only one who ever escaped.

IT IS AN HONOR

It is an honor to walk where all around me stands an earth house made of scarlet, of jet, of ochre, of white shell. It is more than beautiful at the center of the world.

From

In Mad Love
and War

GRACE

for Darlene Wind and James Welch

I think of Wind and her wild ways the year we had nothing to lose and lost it anyway in the cursed country of the fox. We still talk about that winter, how the cold froze imaginary buffalo on the stuffed horizon of snowbanks. The haunting voices of the starved and mutilated broke fences, crashed our thermostat dreams, and we couldn't stand it one more time. So once again we lost a winter in stubborn memory, walked through cheap apartment walls, skated through fields of ghosts into a town that never wanted us, in the epic search for grace.

Like Coyote, like Rabbit, we could not contain our terror and clowned our way through a season of false midnights. We had to swallow that town with laughter, so it would go down easy as honey. And one morning as the sun struggled to break ice, and our dreams had found us with coffee and pancakes in a truck stop along Highway 80, we found grace.

I could say grace was a woman with time on her hands, or a white buffalo escaped from memory. But in that dingy light it was a promise of balance. We once again understood the talk of animals, and spring was lean and hungry with the hope of children and corn.

I would like to say, with grace, we picked ourselves up and walked into the spring thaw. We didn't; the next season was worse. You went home to Leech Lake to work with the tribe and I went south. And, Wind, I am still crazy. I know there is something larger than the memory of a dispossessed people. We have seen it.

DEER DANCER

Nearly everyone had left that bar in the middle of winter except the hardcore. It was the coldest night of the year, every place shut down, but not us. Of course we noticed when she came in. We were Indian ruins. She was the end of beauty. No one knew her, the stranger whose tribe we recognized, her family related to deer, if that's who she was, a people accustomed to hearing songs in pine trees, and making them hearts.

The woman inside the woman who was to dance naked in the bar of misfits blew deer magic. Henry Jack, who could not survive a sober day, thought she was Buffalo Calf Woman come back, passed out, his head by the toilet. All night he dreamed a dream he could not say. The next day he borrowed money, went home, and sent back the money I lent. Now that's a miracle. Some people see vision in a burned tortilla, some in the face of a woman.

This is the bar of broken survivors, the club of shotgun, knife wound, of poison by culture. We who were taught not to stare drank our beer. The players gossiped down their cues. Someone put a quarter in the jukebox to relive despair. Richard's wife dove to kill her. We had to hold her back, empty her pockets of knives and diaper pins, buy her two beers to keep her still, while Richard secretly bought the beauty a drink.

How do I say it? In this language there are no words for how the real world collapses. I could say it in my own and the sacred mounds would come into focus, but I couldn't take it in this dingy envelope. So I look at the stars in this strange city, frozen to the back of the sky, the only promises that ever make sense.

My brother-in-law hung out with white people, went to law school with a perfect record, quit. Says you can keep your laws, your words. And practiced law on the street with his hands. He jimmied to the proverbial dream girl, the face of the moon, while the players racked a new game. He bragged to us, he told her magic words and that's when she broke, became human.

But we all heard his bar voice crack:

What's a girl like you doing in a place like this?

That's what I'd like to know, what are we all doing in a place like this?

You would know she could hear only what she wanted to; don't we all? Left the drink of betrayal Richard bought her, at the bar. What was she on? We all wanted some. Put a quarter in the juke. We all take risks stepping into thin air. Our ceremonies didn't predict this. Or we expected more.

I had to tell you this, for the baby inside the girl sealed up with a lick of hope and swimming into praise of nations. This is not a rooming house, but a dream of winter falls and the deer who portrayed the relatives of strangers. The way back is deer breath on icy windows.

The next dance none of us predicted. She borrowed a chair for the stairway to heaven and stood on a table of names. And danced in the room of children without shoes.

You picked a fine time to leave me, Lucille.
With four hungry children and crops in the field.

And then she took off her clothes. She shook loose memory, waltzed with the empty lover we'd all become.

She was the myth slipped down through dreamtime. The promise of feast we all knew was coming. The deer who crossed through knots of a curse to find us. She was no slouch, and neither were we, watching.

The music ended. And so does the story. I wasn't there. But I imagined her like this, not a stained red dress with tape on her heels but the deer who entered our dream in white dawn, breathed mist into pine trees, her fawn a blessing of meat, the ancestors who never left.

FOR ANNA MAE PICTOU AQUASH, WHOSE SPIRIT IS
PRESENT HERE AND IN THE DAPPLED STARS
(FOR WE REMEMBER THE STORY AND MUST TELL IT
AGAIN SO WE MAY ALL LIVE)

Beneath a sky blurred with mist and wind,
          I am amazed as I watch the violet
heads of crocuses erupt from the stiff earth
          after dying for a season,
as I have watched my own dark head
          appear each morning after entering
the next world
          to come back to this one,
                    amazed.
It is the way in the natural world to understand the place
                              the ghost dancers named
after the heartbreaking destruction.
                    Anna Mae,
                              everything and nothing changes.
You are the shimmering young woman
                    who found her voice,
when you were warned to be silent, or have your body cut away
from you like an elegant weed.
You are the one whose spirit is present in the dappled stars.
(They prance and lope like colored horses who stay with us
          through the streets of these steely cities. And I have seen them
                    nuzzling the frozen bodies of tattered drunks
                    on the corner.)

This morning when the last star is dimming
                    and the buses grind toward
the middle of the city, I know it is ten years since they buried you
the second time in Lakota, a language that could
                                    free you.

I heard about it in Oklahoma, or New Mexico,
how the wind howled and pulled everything down
in a righteous anger.
            (It was the women who told me) and we understood
                        wordlessly
the ripe meaning of your murder.
        As I understand ten years later after the slow changing
                        of the seasons
that we have just begun to touch
        the dazzling whirlwind of our anger,
we have just begun to perceive the amazed world the ghost dancers
        entered
                    crazily, beautifully.

TRICKSTER

Crow, in the new snow.
You caw, caw
             like crazy.
Laugh.
Because you know I'm a fool,
too, like you
skimming over the thin ice
to the war going on
all over the world.

BIRD

The moon plays horn, leaning on the shoulder of the dark universe
to the infinite glitter of chance. Tonight I watched Bird kill himself,

larger than real life. I've always had a theory that some of us
are born with nerve endings longer than our bodies. Out to here,

farther than his convoluted scales could reach. Those nights he
played did he climb the stairway of forgetfulness, with his horn,

a woman who is always beautiful to strangers? All poets
understand the final uselessness of words. We are chords to

other chords to other chords, if we're lucky, to melody. The moon
is brighter than anything I can see when I come out of the theater,

than music, than memory of music, or any mere poem. At least
I can dance to "Ornithology" or sweet-talk beside "Charlie's Blues,"

but inside this poem I can't play a horn, hijack a plane to
somewhere where music is the place those nerve endings dangle.

Each rhapsody embodies counterpoint, and pain stuns the woman
in high heels, the man behind the horn, sings the heart.

To survive is sometimes a leap into madness. The fingers of
saints are still hot from miracles, but can they save themselves?

Where is the dimension a god lives who will take Bird home?
I want to see it, I said to the Catalinas, to the Rincons,

to anyone listening in the dark. I said, Let me hear you
by any means: by horn, by fever, by night, even by some poem

attempting flight home.

THE REAL REVOLUTION IS LOVE

I argue with Roberto on the slick-tiled patio
where houseplants as big as elms sway in a samba
breeze at four or five in the Managua morning
after too many yerbabuenas and as many shots of
golden rum. And watch Pedro follow Diane up
her brown arm, over the shoulder of her cool dress,
the valleys of her neck to the place inside her
ear where he isn't speaking revolution. And Alonzo
tosses in the rhetoric made of too much rum and
the burden of being an American in a country
he no longer belongs to.

What we are dealing with here are ideological
differences, political power, he says to
impress a woman who is gorgeously intelligent
and who reminds me of the soft oasis
of my lover's cheek. She doesn't believe
anything but the language of damp earth
beneath a banana tree at noon, and will soon
disappear in the screen of rum, with a man
who keeps his political secrets to himself
in favor of love.

I argue with Roberto, and laugh across the
continent to Diane, who is on the other side
of the flat, round table whose surface ships

would fall off if they sailed to the other
side. *We are Anishnabe* and *Muscogee.*
We have wars of our own.
Knowing this we laugh and laugh,
until she disappears into the poinsettia forest
with Pedro, who is still arriving from Puerto Rico.
Palm trees flutter in smoldering tongues.
I can look through the houses, the wind, and hear
quick laughter become a train
that has no name. Columbus doesn't leave
the bow of the slippery ship.

*This is the land of revolution. You can do anything
 you want*, Roberto tries to persuade me. I fight my way
through the cloud of rum and laughter, through lines
of Spanish and spirits of the recently dead whose elbows
rustle the palm leaves. It is almost dawn and we are still
a long way from morning, but never far enough
to get away.

I do what I want, and take my revolution to bed with
me, alone. And awake in a story told by my ancestors
when they speak a version of the very beginning,
of how so long ago we climbed the backbone of these
tortuous Americas. I listen to the splash of the Atlantic
and Pacific and see Columbus land once more,
over and over again.

This is not a foreign country, but the land of our dreams.

I listen to the gunfire we cannot hear, and begin
this journey with the light of knowing
the root of my own furious love.

SONG FOR THE DEER AND MYSELF TO RETURN ON

This morning when I looked out the roof window
before dawn and a few stars were still caught
in the fragile weft of ebony night
I was overwhelmed. I sang the song Louis taught me:
a song to call the deer in Creek, when hunting,
and I am certainly hunting something as magic as deer
in this city far from the hammock of my mother's belly.
It works, of course, and deer came into this room
and wondered at finding themselves
in a house near downtown Denver.
Now the deer and I are trying to figure out a song
to get them back, to get all of us back,
because if it works I'm going with them.
And it's too early to call Louis
and nearly too late to go home.

for Louis Oliver

RAINY DAWN

I can still close my eyes and open them four floors up looking south and west from the hospital, the approximate direction of Acoma, and farther on to the roofs of the houses of the gods who have learned there are no endings, only beginnings. That day so hot, heat danced in waves off bright car tops, we both stood poised at that door from the east, listened for a long time to the sound of our grandmothers' voices, the brushing wind of sacred wings, the rattle of raindrops in dry gourds. I had to participate in the dreaming of you into memory, cupped your head in the bowl of my body as ancestors lined up to give you a name made of their dreams cast once more into this stew of precious spirit and flesh. And let you go, as I am letting you go once more in this ceremony of the living. And when you were born I held you wet and unfolding, like a butterfly newly born from the chrysalis of my body. And breathed with you as you breathed your first breath. Then was your promise to take it on like the rest of us, this immense journey, for love, for rain.

SANTA FE

The wind blows lilacs out of the east. And it isn't lilac season. And I
am walking the street in front of St. Francis Cathedral in Santa Fe.
Oh, and it's a few years earlier and more. That's how you tell real
time. It is here, it is there. The lilacs have taken over everything: the
sky, the narrow streets, my shoulders, my lips. I talk lilac. And there
is nothing else until a woman the size of a fox breaks through the
bushes, breaks the purple web. She is tall and black and gorgeous.
She is the size of a fox on the arm of a white man who looks and
tastes like cocaine. She lies for cocaine, dangles on the arm of
cocaine. And lies to me now from a room in the DeVargas Hotel,
where she has eaten her lover, white powder on her lips. That is true
now; it is not true anymore. Eventually space curves, walks over and
taps me on the shoulder. On the sidewalk I stand near St. Francis;
he has been bronzed, a perpetual tan, with birds on his hand, his
shoulder, deer at his feet. I am Indian and in this town I will never
be a saint. I am seventeen and shy and wild. I have been up until
three at a party, but there is no woman in the DeVargas Hotel, for
that story hasn't yet been invented. A man whose face I will never
remember, and never did, drives up on a Harley-Davidson. There are
lilacs on his arm; they spill out from the spokes of his wheels. He
wants me on his arm, on the back of his lilac bike touring the flower
kingdom of San Francisco. And for a piece of time the size of a
nickel, I think, maybe. But maybe is vapor, has no anchor here in the
sun beneath St. Francis Cathedral. And space is as solid as the
bronze statue of St. Francis, the fox breaking through the lilacs, my
invention of this story, the wind blowing.

DESIRE

Say I chew desire and water is an explosion
of sugar wings in my mouth.

Say it tastes of you.

Say I could drown because you left
for the time it takes a blackbird to understand
a pine tree.

Say we enter the pine woods at dawn.

We never slept and the only opium we smoked
was what became of our mingled breath.

Say the stars have never learned
to say good-bye.

Say all of this is true and more

than there are blackbirds
in a heaven of blackbirds.

for J.

THE BOOK OF MYTHS

When I entered the book of myths
      in your sandalwood room on the granite island,
I did not ask for a way out.
This is not the century for false pregnancy
           in these times when myths
                  have taken to the streets.
There is no more imagination; we are in it now, girl.
      We traveled the stolen island of Manhattan
           in a tongue of wind off the Atlantic
    shaking our shells, in our mad skins.
I did not tell you when I saw Rabbit sobbing and laughing
          as he shook his dangerous bag of tricks
    into the mutiny world on that street outside Hunter.
Out came you and me blinking our eyes once more, entwined in
  our loves
      and hates as we set off to recognize the sweet
and bitter gods who walk beside us, whisper madness
in our invisible ears any ordinary day.
I have fallen in love a thousand times over; every day is a common
miracle of salt roses, of fire in the prophecy wind, and now and then
      I taste the newborn blood in my daughter's
          silk hair, as if she were not nearly a woman
    brown and electric in her nearly womanly self.
There is a Helen in every language; in American her name is Marilyn
        but in my subversive country,
    she is dark earth and round and full of names

dressed in bodies of women
    who enter and leave the knife wounds of this terrifyingly
beautiful land.
    In the book of myths that fell open in your room of unicorns

I did not imagine the fiery goddess in the middle of the island.
She is a sweet trick of flame,
    had everyone dancing, laughing, and telling the stories
that unglue the talking spirit from the pages.
When the dawn light came on through the windows,
            I understood how my bones would one day
    stand up, brush off the lovely skin like a satin blouse,
and dance with foolish grace to heaven.

TRANSFORMATIONS

This poem is a letter to tell you that I have smelled the hatred you have tried to find me with; you would like to destroy me. Bone splintered in the eye of one you choose to name your enemy won't make it better for you to see. It could take a thousand years if you name it that way, but then, to see after all that time, never could anything be so clear. Memory has many forms. When I think of early winter I think of a blackbird laughing in the frozen air; guards a piece of light. (I saw the whole world caught in that sound, the sun stopped for a moment because of tough belief.) I don't know what that has to do with what I am trying to tell you except that I know you can turn a poem into something else. This poem could be a bear treading the far northern tundra, smelling the air for sweet alive meat. Or a piece of seaweed stumbling in the sea. Or a blackbird, laughing. What I mean is that hatred can be turned into something else, if you have the right words, the right meanings, buried in that tender place in your heart where the most precious animals live. Down the street an ambulance has come to rescue an old man who is slowly losing his life. Not many can see that he is already becoming the backyard tree he has tended for years, before he moves on. He is not sad, but compassionate for the fears moving around him.

That's what I mean to tell you. On the other side of the place you live stands a dark woman. She has been trying to talk to you for years. You have called the same name in the middle of a nightmare, from the center of miracles. She is beautiful.
This is your hatred back. She loves you.

EAGLE POEM

To pray you open your whole self
To sky, to earth, to sun, to moon
To one whole voice that is you.
And know there is more
That you can't see, can't hear,
Can't know except in moments
Steadily growing, and in languages
That aren't always sound but other
Circles of motion.
Like eagle that Sunday morning
Over Salt River. Circled in blue sky
In wind, swept our hearts clean
With sacred wings.
We see you, see ourselves and know
That we must take the utmost care
And kindness in all things.
Breathe in, knowing we are made of
All this, and breathe, knowing
We are truly blessed because we
Were born, and die soon within a
True circle of motion,
Like eagle rounding out the morning
Inside us.
We pray that it will be done
In beauty.
In beauty.

From
The Woman
Who Fell
from the Sky

RECONCILIATION, A PRAYER

I.

We gather at the shore of all knowledge as peoples who were put
here by a god who wanted relatives.

This god was lonely for touch, and imagined herself as a woman,
with children to suckle, to sing with—to continue the web of the
terrifyingly beautiful cosmos of her womb.

This god became a father who wished for others to walk beside him
in the belly of creation.

This god laughed and cried with us as a sister at the sweet tragedy of
our predicament—foolish humans

Or built a fire, as our brother to keep us warm.

This god who grew to love us became our lover, sharing tables of
food enough for everyone in this whole world.

II.

Oh sun, moon, stars, our other relatives peering at us from the inside
of god's house walk with us as we climb into the next century
naked but for the stories we have of each other. Keep us from giving
up in this land of nightmares which is also the land of miracles.

We sing our song which we've been promised has no beginning or
end.

III.

All acts of kindness are lights in the war for justice.

IV.

We gather up these strands broken from the web of life. They shiver with our love, as we call them the names of our relatives and carry them to our home made of the four directions and sing:

Of the south, where we feasted and were given new clothes.

Of the west, where we gave up the best of us to the stars as food for the battle.

Of the north, where we cried because we were forsaken by our dreams.

Of the east because returned to us is the spirit of all that we love.

in memory of Audre Lorde, for her memorial at the Cathedral Church of St. John the Divine, 1993

THE CREATION STORY

I'm not afraid of love
or its consequence of light.

It's not easy to say this
or anything when my entrails
dangle between paradise
and fear.

I am ashamed
I never had the words
to carry a friend from her death
to the stars
correctly.

Or the words to keep
my people safe
from drought
or gunshot.

The stars who were created by words
are circling over this house
formed of calcium, of blood

this house
in danger of being torn apart
by stones of fear.

If these words can do anything
if these songs can do anything
I say bless this house
with stars.

Transfix us with love.

THE WOMAN WHO FELL FROM THE SKY

Once a woman fell from the sky. The woman who fell from the sky was neither a murderer nor a saint. She was rather ordinary, though beautiful in her walk, like one who has experienced freedom from earth's gravity. When I see her I think of an antelope grazing the alpine meadows in mountains whose names are as ancient as the sound that created the first world.

Saint Coincidence thought he recognized her as she began falling toward him from the sky in a slow spin, like the spiral of events marking an ascension of grace. There was something in the curve of her shoulder, a familiar slope that led him into the lightest moment of his life.

He could not bear it and turned to ask a woman in high heels for a quarter. She was of the family of myths who would give everything if asked. She looked like all the wives he'd lost. And he had nothing to lose anymore in this city of terrible paradox where a woman was falling toward him from the sky.

The strange beauty in heels disappeared from the path of Saint Coincidence, with all her money held tightly in her purse, into the glass of advertisements. Saint Coincidence shuffled back onto the ice to watch the woman falling and falling.

Saint Coincidence, who was not a saint, perhaps a murderer if you count the people he shot without knowing during the stint that took his mind in Vietnam or Cambodia—remembered the girl he yearned to love when they were kids at Indian boarding school.

He could still see her on the dusty playground, off in the distance, years to the west past the icy parking lot of the Safeway. She was a blurred vision of the bittersweet and this memory had forced him to live through the violence of fire.

There they stood witness together to strange acts of cruelty by strangers, as well as the surprise of rare kindnesses.

The woman who was to fall from the sky was the girl with skinned knees whose spirit knew how to climb to the stars. Once she told him the stars spoke a language akin to the plains of her home, a language like rocks.

He watched her once make the ascent, after a severe beating. No one could touch the soul masked by name, age, and tribal affiliation. Myth was as real as a scalp being scraped for lice.

Lila also dreamed of a love not disturbed by the wreck of culture she was forced to attend. It sprang up here and there like miraculous flowers in the cracks of the collision. It was there she found Johnny, who didn't have a saint's name when he showed up for school. He understood the journey and didn't make fun of her for her peculiar ways, despite the risks.

Johnny was named Johnny by the priests because his Indian name was foreign to their European tongues. He named himself Saint Coincidence many years later after he lost himself in drink in a city he'd been sent to to learn a trade. Maybe you needed English to know how to pray in the city. He could speak a fractured English. His own language had become a baby language to him, made of the comforting voice of his grandmother as she taught him to be a human.

Johnny had been praying for years and had finally given up on a god who appeared to give up on him. Then one night as he tossed pennies on the sidewalk with his cousin and another lost traveler, he prayed to Coincidence and won. The event demanded a new name. He gave himself the name Saint Coincidence.

His ragged life gleamed with possibility until a ghost-priest brushed by him as he walked the sidewalk looking for a job to add to his stack of new luck. The priest appeared to look through to the boy in him. He despaired. He would always be a boy on his knees, the burden of shame rooting him.

Saint Coincidence went back to wandering without a home in the maze of asphalt. Asphalt could be a pathway toward God, he reasoned, though he'd always imagined the road he took with his brothers when they raised sheep as children. Asphalt had led him here to the Safeway where a woman was falling from the sky.

The memory of all time relative to Lila and Johnny was seen by an abandoned cat washing herself next to the aluminum-can bin of the grocery store.

These humans set off strange phenomena, she thought and made no attachment to the thought. It was what it was, this event, shimmering there between the frozen parking lot of the store and the sky, something unusual and yet quite ordinary.

Like the sun falling fast in the west, this event carried particles of light through the trees.

Some say God is a murderer for letting children and saints slip through his or her hands. Some call God a father of saints or a mother of demons. Lila had seen God and could tell you God was neither male nor female and made of absolutely everything of beauty, of wordlessness.

This unnameable thing of beauty is what shapes a flock of birds who know exactly when to turn together in flight in the winds used to make words. Everyone turns together though we may not see each other stacked in the invisible dimensions.

This is what Lila saw, she told Johnny once. The sisters called it blasphemy.

Johnny ran away from boarding school the first winter with his two brothers, who'd run away before. His brothers wrapped Johnny Boy, as they called him, with their bodies to keep him warm. They froze and became part of the stars.

Johnny didn't make it home either. The school officials took him back the next day. To mourn his brothers would be to admit an unspeakable pain, so he became an athlete who ran faster than any record ever made in the history of the school, faster than the tears.

Lila never forgot about Johnny, who left school to join the army, and a few years later as she walked home from her job at Dairy Queen she made a turn in the road.

Call it destiny or coincidence—but the urge to fly was as strong as the need to push when at the precipice of any birth. It was what led her into the story told before she'd grown ears to hear, as she turned from stone to fish to human in her mother's belly.

Once, the stars made their way down stairs of ice to the earth to find mates. Some of the women were angry at their inattentive husbands, bored, or frustrated with the cycle of living and dying. They ran off with the stars, as did a few who saw their chance for travel and enlightenment.

They weren't heard from for years, until one of the women returned. She dared to look back and fell. Fell through centuries, through the beauty of the night sky, made a hole in a rock near the place Lila's mother had been born. She took up where she had left off, with her children from the stars. She was remembered.

This story was Lila's refuge those nights she'd prayed on her knees with the other children in the school dorms. It was too painful to miss her mother.

A year after she'd graduated and worked cleaning house during the day, and evenings at the Dairy Queen, she laughed to think of herself wearing her uniform spotted with sweets and milk, as she left on the arms of one of the stars. Surely she could find love in a place that did not know the disturbance of fear.

While Lila lived in the sky she gave birth to three children and they made her happy. Though she had lost conscious memory of the place before, a song climbed up her legs from far away, to the rooms of her heart.

Later she would tell Johnny it was the sound of destiny, which is similar to a prayer reaching out to claim her.

You can't ignore these things, she would tell him, and it led her to the place her husband had warned her was too sacred for women.

She carried the twins in her arms as her daughter grabbed her skirt in her small fists. She looked into the forbidden place and leaped.

She fell and was still falling when Saint Coincidence caught her in his arms in front of the Safeway as he made a turn from borrowing spare change from strangers.

The children crawled safely from their mother. The cat stalked a bit of flying trash set into motion by the wave of falling

or the converse wave of gathering together.

THE FLOOD

It had been years since I'd seen the watermonster, the snake who lived at the bottom of the lake. He had disappeared in the age of reason, as a mystery that never happened.

For in the muggy lake was the girl I could have been at sixteen, wrested from the torment of exaggerated fools, one version anyway, though the story at the surface would say car accident, or drowning while drinking, all of it eventually accidental.

This story is not an accident, nor is the existence of the watersnake in the memory of the people as they carried the burden of the myth from Alabama to Oklahoma. Each reluctant step pounded memory into the broken heart and no one will ever forget it.

When I walk the stairway of water into the abyss, I return as the wife of the watermonster, in a blanket of time decorated with swatches of cloth and feathers from our favorite clothes.

The stories of the battles of the watersnake are forever ongoing, and those stories soaked into my blood since infancy like deer gravy, so how could I resist the watersnake, who appeared as the most handsome man in the tribe, or any band whose visits I'd been witness to since childhood?

This had been going on for centuries: the first time he appeared I carried my baby sister on my back as I went to get water. She laughed at a woodpecker flitting like a small sun above us and before I could deter the symbol we were in it.

My body was already on fire with the explosion of womanhood as if I were flint, hot stone, and when he stepped out of the water he was the first myth I had ever seen uncovered. I had surprised him in a human moment—I looked aside but I could not discount what I had seen.

My baby sister's cry pinched reality, the woodpecker a warning of a disjuncture in the brimming sky, and then a man who was not a man but a myth.

What I had seen there were no words for except in the sacred language of the most holy recounting, so when I ran back to the village, drenched in salt, how could I explain the water jar left empty by the river to my mother who deciphered my burning lips as shame?

My imagination swallowed me like a mica sky, but I had seen the watermonster in the fight of lightning storms, breaking trees, stirring up killing winds, and had lost my favorite brother to a spear of the sacred flame, so certainly I would know my beloved if he were hidden in the blushing skin of the suddenly vulnerable.

I was taken with a fever and nothing cured it until I dreamed my fiery body dipped in the river where it fed into the lake. My father carried me as if I were newborn, as if he were presenting me once more to the world, and when he dipped me I was quenched, pronounced healed.

My parents immediately made plans to marry me to an important man who was years older but would provide me with everything I needed to survive in this world, a world I could no longer perceive, as I had been blinded with a ring of water when I was most in need of a drink by a snake who was not a snake, and how did he know my absolute secrets, those created at the brink of acquired language?

When I disappeared it was in a storm that destroyed the houses of my relatives. My baby sister was found sucking on her hand in the crook of an oak.

And though it may have appeared otherwise, I did not go willingly. That night I had seen my face strung on the shell belt of my ancestors, and I was standing next to a man who could not look me in the eye.

The oldest woman in the tribe wanted to remember me as a symbol in the story of a girl who disobeyed, who gave in to her desires before marriage and was destroyed by the monster disguised as the seductive warrior.

Others saw the car I was driving as it drove into the lake early one morning, the time the carriers of tradition wake up, before the sun or the approach of woodpeckers, and found the emptied six-pack on the sandy shores of the lake.

The power of the victim is a power that will always be reckoned with, one way or the other. When the proverbial sixteen-year-old woman walked down to the lake within her were all sixteen-year-old women who had questioned their power from time immemorial.

Her imagination was larger than the small frame house at the north edge of town, with the broken cars surrounding it like a necklace of futility, larger than the town itself leaning into the lake. Nothing could stop it, just as no one could stop the bearing-down thunderheads as they gathered overhead in the war of opposites.

Years later when she walked out of the lake and headed for town, no one recognized her, or themselves, in the drench of fire and rain. The watersnake was a story no one told anymore. They'd entered a drought that no one recognized as drought, the convenience store a signal of temporary amnesia.

I had gone out to get bread, eggs, and the newspaper before breakfast and hurried the cashier for my change as the crazy woman walked in, for I could not see myself as I had abandoned her some twenty years ago in a blue windbreaker at the edge of the man-made lake as everyone dove naked and drunk off the sheer cliff, as if we had nothing to live for, not then or ever.

It was beginning to rain in Oklahoma, the rain that would flood the world.

A POSTCOLONIAL TALE

Every day is a reenactment of the creation story. We emerge from dense unspeakable material, through the shimmering power of dreaming stuff.

This is the first world, and the last.

Once we abandoned ourselves for television, the box that separates the dreamer from the dreaming. It was as if we were stolen, put into a bag carried on the back of a white man who pretends to own the earth and the sky. In the sack were all the people of the world. We fought until there was a hole in the bag.

When we fell we were not aware of falling. We were driving to work, or to the mall. The children were in school learning subtraction with guns.

We found ourselves somewhere near the diminishing point of civilization, not far from the trickster's bag of tricks. Everything was as we imagined it. The earth and stars, every creature and leaf imagined with us.

When we fell we were not aware of falling. We were driving to work or to the mall. The children were in school learning subtraction with guns.

The imagining needs praise as does any living thing.
We are evidence of this praise.
And when we laugh, we're indestructible.
No story or song will translate
the full impact of falling,
or the inverse power of rising up.
Of rising up.

Our children put down their guns when we did to imagine with us.
We imagined the shining link between the heart and the sun.
We imagined tables of food for everyone.
We imagined the songs.

The imagination conversely illumines us, speaks with us, sings with
us, drums with us, loves us.

THE MYTH OF BLACKBIRDS

The hours we counted precious were blackbirds in the density of Washington. Taxis toured the labyrinth with passengers of mist as the myth of ancient love took the shape of two figures carrying the dawn tenderly on their shoulders to the shores of the Potomac.

We fled the drama of lit marble in the capital for a refuge held up by sweet, everlasting earth. The man from Ghana who wheeled our bags was lonesome for his homeland, but commerce made it necessary to carry someone else's burdens. The stars told me how to find us in this disorder of systems.

Washington did not ever sleep that night in the sequence of eternal nights. There were whirring calculators, computers stealing names, while spirits of the disappeared drank coffee at an all-night cafe in this city of disturbed relativity.

Justice is a story by heart in the beloved country where imagination weeps. The sacred mountains only appear to be asleep. When we finally found the room in the hall of mirrors and shut the door I could no longer bear the beauty of scarlet licked with yellow on the wings of blackbirds.

This is the world in which we undressed together. Within it white deer intersect with the wisdom of the hunter of grace. Horses wheel toward the morning star. Memory was always more than paper and cannot be broken by violent history or stolen by thieves of childhood. We cannot be separated in the loop of mystery between blackbirds and the memory of blackbirds.

And in the predawn when we had slept for centuries in a drenching sweet rain you touched me and the springs of clear water beneath my skin were new knowledge. And I loved you in this city of death.

Through the darkness in the sheer rise of clipped green grass and asphalt our ancestors appear together at the shoreline of the Potomac in their moccasins and pressed suits of discreet armor. They go to the water from the cars of smokey trains, or dismount from horses dusty with fatigue.

See the children who became our grandparents, the old ones whose bones fertilize the corn. They form us in our sleep of exhaustion as we make our way through this world of skewed justice, of songs without singers.

I embrace these spirits of relatives who always return to the place of beauty, whatever the outcome in the spiral of power. And I particularly admire the tender construction of your spine which in the gentle dawning is a ladder between the deep in which stars are perfectly stars, and the heavens where we converse with eagles.

And I am thankful to the brutal city for the space which outlines your limber beauty. To the man from Ghana who also loves the poetry of the stars. To the ancestors who do not forget us in the concrete and paper illusion. To the blackbirds who are exactly blackbirds. And to you sweetheart as we make our incredible journey.

THE SONG OF THE HOUSE IN THE HOUSE

I've seen a ghost house in the street
loom up behind a man with lice wearing a blanket
who was someone I loved, a father or a brother.

Do you know how it is to hold on to anything in the dark,
said the man who was the child of unspoken wishes
rattling the toys in the ghost house?

The velocity of fear overtakes the spin of a warring planet,
and the scent of urine reminds the house of the child in diapers
who fell asleep to the sound of his mother rustling
the sheets while evil took a turn in the house.

The sound emphasized songlessness
of a mother who could not watch and turned on the
television. She slept and slept while
the children grew in the house that slanted
toward the thing devouring it.

There's no easy way to know this thing, said the man
who grew smaller in the shadow of the house as it leaned over
to smell the tender neck of the child as he sipped
wine with other strangers.

When the earth makes a particularly hard turn
someone can fall off—a house can tilt
toward the street or ride the hip of destruction.

To maneuver deftly can mean learning another angle
of motion to take the place of wine
and other spirits caught by shiny glass or powder
attracted by the wound of those who once knew how to sing,

I'm sorry, said the house who sat down by the man
who'd taken refuge in the street.

The inhabitants could be heard disappearing
through aluminum walls as the boy bent
to the slap and beating by the father who was charged
with loving and nothing in him could answer to that angel.

I could not protect you, cried the house:

Though the house gleamed with appliances.
Though the house was built with postwar money
and hope.
Though the house was their haven after the war.
Though the war never ended.

LETTER FROM THE END OF
THE TWENTIETH CENTURY

I shared a half hour of my life this morning with Rammi, an Igbo man from northern Nigeria who drove me in his taxi to the airport. Chicago rose up as a mechanical giant with soft insides buzzing around to keep it going. We were part of the spin.

Rammi told the story of his friend, who one morning around seven— a morning much like this one—was filling his taxi with gas. He was imagining home, a village whose memories had given him sustenance to study through his degree and would keep him going one more year until he had the money he needed to return.

As the sun broke through the gray morning he heard his mother tell him, the way she had told him when he was a young boy, how the sun had once been an Igbo and returned every morning to visit relatives.

These memories were the coat that kept him warm on the streets of ice.

He was interrupted by a young man who asked him for money, a young man who was like many he saw on his daily journey onto the street to collect fares. "Oh no, sorry man. I don't have anything I can give you," he said as he patted the pockets of his worn slacks, his thin nylon jacket.

He turned back to the attention of filling his gas tank. What a beautiful morning, almost warm. And the same sun, the same Igbo looking down on him in the streets of the labyrinth far far from home.

And just like that he was gone, from a gunshot wound at the back of his head—the hit of a casual murderer.

As we near the concrete plains of O'Hare, I imagine the spirit of Rammi's friend at the door of his mother's house, the bag of dreams in his hands dripping with blood. His mother's tears make a river of red stars to an empty moon.

The whole village mourns with her. The ritual of tears and drums summon the ancestors who carry his spirit into the next world.

There he can still hear the drums of his relatives as they accompany him on his journey.
He must settle the story of his murder
or he will come back a ghost.

The smallest talking drum is an insistent heart, leads his spirit to the killer, a young Jamaican immigrant who was traced to his apartment because his shirt of blood was found by the police, thrown off in the alley with his driver's license in the pocket.

He searches for his murderer in the bowels of Chicago and finds him shivering in a cramped jail cell. He could hang him or knife him and it would be called suicide. It would be the easiest thing.

But his mother's grief moves his heart. He hears the prayers of the young man's mother. There is always a choice, even after death.

He gives the young man his favorite name and calls him his brother. The young killer is then no longer shamed but filled with remorse and cries all the cries he has stored for a thousand years. He learns to love himself as he never could, because his enemy, who has every reason to destroy him, loves him.

That's the story that follows me everywhere and won't let me sleep: from Tallahassee Grounds to Chicago, to my home near the Rio Grande.

It sustains me through these tough distances.

PROMISE OF BLUE HORSES

A blue horse turns into a streak of lightning,
>   then the sun—
relating the difference between sadness
>   and the need to praise
that which makes us joyful. I can't calculate
>   how the earth tips hungrily
toward the sun—then soaks up rain—or the density
>   of this unbearable need
to be next to you. It's a palpable thing—this earth philosophy
>   and familiar in the dark
like your skin under my hand. We are a small earth. It's no
>   simple thing. Eventually
we will be dust together, can be used to make a house, to stop
>   a flood or grow food
for those who will never remember who we were, or know
>   that we loved fiercely.
Laughter and sadness eventually become the same song turning us
>   toward the nearest star—
a star constructed of eternity and elements of dust barely visible
>   in the twilight as you travel
east. I run with the blue horses of electricity who surround
>   the heart
and imagine a promise made when no promise was possible.

THE PLACE THE MUSICIAN BECAME A BEAR

for Jim Pepper

I think of the lush stillness of the end of a world, sung into place by
singers and the rattle of turtles in the dark morning.

When embers from the sacred middle are climbing out the other side of stars.

When the moon has stomp-danced with us from one horizon to the next,
such a soft awakening.

Our souls imitate lights in the Milky Way. We've always known where to go to
become ourselves again in the human comedy.

It's the how that baffles. A saxophone can complicate things.

You knew this, as do all musicians when the walk becomes a
necessary dance to fuel the fool heart,

Or the single complicated human becomes a wave of humanness and forgets
to be ashamed of making the wrong step.

I'm talking about an early morning in Brooklyn, the streets the color of ashes,
do you see the connection?

It's not as if the stars forsake us, we forget about them, or remake the pattern
in a field of white crystal or of some other tricky fate.

We never mistook ourselves for anything but human.

The wings of the Milky Way lead back to the singers.
And there's the saxophone again.

It's about rearranging the song to include the subway hiss
under your feet in Brooklyn.

And the laugh of a bear who thought he was a human.

As he plays that tune again, the one about the wobble of the earth
spinning so damned hard

it hurts.

FISHING

This is the longest day of the year, on the Illinois River or a similar river in the same place. Cicadas are part of the song as they praise their invisible ancestors while fish blinking back the relentless sun in Oklahoma circle in the muggy river of life. They dare the fisher to come and get them. Fish, too, anticipate the game of fishing. Their ancestors perfected the moves, sent down stories that appear as electrical impulses when sunlight hits water. The hook carries great symbology in the coming of age, and is crucial to the making of warriors. The greatest warriors are those who dangle a human for hours on a string, break sacred water for the profanity of air, then snap fiercely back into pearly molecules that describe fishness.

They smell me as I walk the banks with fishing pole, night crawlers, and a promise I made to that old friend Louis to fish with him this summer. This is the only place I can keep that promise, inside a poem as familiar to him as the banks of his favorite fishing place. I try not to let the fish see me see them as they look for his tracks on the soft earth made of fossils and ashes. I hear the burble of fish talk: *When is that old Creek coming back? He was the one we loved to tease most, we liked his songs and once in a while he gave us a good run.*

Last night I dreamed I tried to die. I was going to look for Louis. It was rather comical. I worked hard to muster my last breath, then lay down in the summer, along the banks of the last mythic river, my pole and tackle box next to me. What I thought was my last breath floated off as a cloud making an umbrella of grief over my relatives. How embarrassing when the next breath came, and then the next. I reeled in one after another, as if I'd caught a bucket of suckers instead of bass. I guess it wasn't my time, I explained, and went fishing anyway as a liar and I know most fishers to be liars most of the time. Even Louis when it came to fishing, or even dying.

The leap between the sacred and profane is as thin as fishing line, and is part of the mystery on this river of life, as is the way our people continue to make warriors in the strangest of times. I save this part of the poem for the fish camp next to the oldest spirits whose dogs bark to greet visitors. It's near Louis's favorite spot, where the wisest and fattest fish laze. I'll meet him there.

PROMISE

for Krista Rae Chico

The guardians of dusk blow fire from the Rincons as clouds confer over the Catalinas in the fading tracks of humans. I interpret the blur of red as female rain tomorrow, or the child born with the blessings of animals who will always protect her.

I am always amazed at the skill of rain clouds who outline the weave of human density. Crickets memorize the chance event with rainsongs they have practiced for centuries. I am recreated by that language. Their predictions are always true. And as beautiful as saguaro flowers drinking rain.

I see the moon as I have never seen the moon, a half shell, just large enough for a cradleboard and the child who takes part in the dance of evolution as seen in the procession of tadpoles to humans painting the walls with wishes.

From the moon we all look the same.

In two days the girl will be born and nothing will ever look the same. I knew the monsoon clouds were talking about it as they softened the speed of light.

You can manipulate words to turn departure into aperture, but you cannot figure the velocity of love and how it enters every equation.

It's related to the calculation of the speed of light, and how light prevails.

And then the evening star nods her head, nearby a lone jet ascending. I understand how light prevails. And when she was born it rained. Everything came true the way it was promised.

THE DAWN APPEARS WITH BUTTERFLIES

You leave before daybreak to prepare your husband's body for burial at dawn. It is one of countless dawns since the first crack of consciousness, each buried in molecular memory, each as distinct as your face in the stew of human faces, your eyes blinking back force in the vortex of loss and heartbreak.

I put on another pot of coffee, watch out the kitchen window at the beginning of the world, follow your difficult journey to Flagstaff, through rocks that recall the scarlet promises of gods, their interminable journeys, and pine. Until I can no longer see, but continue to believe in the sun's promise to return:

And it will this morning. And tomorrow. And the day after tomorrow, building the spiral called eternity out of each sun, the dance of butterflies evoking the emerging.

Two nights ago you drove north from the hospital at Flagstaff, after his abandonment to the grace we pursue as wild horses the wind. Your grief was the dark outlining the stars. One star in particular waved to you as you maneuvered in the nightmare of the myth of death. It broke loose, stammered, then flew marking the place between the star house of the gods and Third Mesa.

You laughed with the spirit of your husband who would toss stars! And your tears made a pale butterfly, the color of dawn, which is the color of the sky of the next world, which isn't that far away.

There is no tear in the pattern. It is perfect, as our gradual return to the maker of butterflies, or our laughter as we considered the joke of burying him in the shirt you always wanted him to wear, a shirt he hated.

Someone is singing in the village. And the sacredness of all previous dawns resonates. That is the power of the singer who respects the power of the place without words, which is as butterflies, returning to the sun, our star in the scheme of stars, of revolving worlds.

And within that the power of the dying is to know when to make that perfect leap into everything. We are all dying together, though there is nothing like the loneliness of being the first or the last, and we all take that place with each other.

In the west at every twilight since the beginning, the oldest spirits camp out with their dogs. It is always in the season just before winter. It is always shooting star weather and they wash dishes by dipping them in river water warmed in a buckct.

Coffee heats over the fire. Crows take their sacred place. The sun always returns and butterflies are a memory of one loved like no other. All events in the universe are ordinary. Even miracles occur ordinarily as spirits travel to the moon, visit distant relatives, as always.

Then at dusk they share the fire that warms the world, and sit together remembering everything, recounting the matrix of allies and enemies, of sons and daughters, of lovers and lovers, each molecule of the sky and earth an explosion of memory within us.

In this fierce drama of everything we are at this juncture of our linked journey to the Milky Way—as your babies stir in bittersweet dreams while you travel to your most difficult good-bye—as Grandma lies down with them to comfort them—as your father's truck starts down the road in the village as a dog barks

everything is a prayer for this journey.
As you shut the door behind you in the dark:
Wings of dusk
Wings of night sky
Wings of dawn
Wings of morning light

It is sunrise now.

PERHAPS THE WORLD ENDS HERE

The world begins at a kitchen table. No matter what, we must eat to live.

The gifts of earth are brought and prepared, set on the table. So it has been since creation, and it will go on.

We chase chickens or dogs away from it. Babies teethe at the corners. They scrape their knees under it.

It is here that children are given instructions on what it means to be human. We make men at it, we make women.

At this table we gossip, recall enemies and the ghosts of lovers.

Our dreams drink coffee with us as they put their arms around our children. They laugh with us at our poor falling-down selves and as we put ourselves back together once again at the table.

This table has been a house in the rain, an umbrella in the sun.

Wars have begun and ended at this table. It is a place to hide in the shadow of terror. A place to celebrate the terrible victory.

We have given birth on this table, and have prepared our parents for burial here.

At this table we sing with joy, with sorrow. We pray of suffering and remorse. We give thanks.

Perhaps the world will end at the kitchen table, while we are laughing and crying, eating of the last sweet bite.

From

A Map to the
Next World:
Poems and Tales

SONGLINE OF DAWN

We are ascending through the dawn
the sky, blushed with the fever
                              of attraction.
I don't want to leave my daughter,
                              or the babies.
I can see their house, a refuge in the dark near the university.
Protect them, oh gods of the scarlet light
who love us fiercely despite our acts of stupidity
our utter failings.
May this morning light be food for their bones,
for their spirits dressed
                              in manes of beautiful black hair
in skins the color of the earth as it meets the sky.
Higher we fly over the valley of monster bones
left scattered in the dirt to remind us that breathing
is rooted somewhere other than the lungs.
                              My spirit approaches with reverence
because it harbors the story, of how these beloveds
                              appeared to fail
then climbed into the sky to stars of indigo.
                  And we keep going past the laughter and tears
of the babies who will grow up to become a light field
just beyond us.
And then the sun breaks over the yawning mountain.
And the plane shivers as we dip toward
                              an old volcanic field.

127

It is still smoldering
motivated by the love of one deity for another.
It's an old story and we're in it so deep we have become them.
The sun leans on one elbow after making love
                    savoring the wetlands just off the freeway.
We are closer to the gods than we ever thought possible.

A MAP TO THE NEXT WORLD

for Desiray Kierra Chee

In the last days of the fourth world I wished to make a map for
those who would climb through the hole in the sky.

My only tools were the desires of humans as they emerged
from the killing fields, from the bedrooms and the kitchens.

For the soul is a wanderer with many hands and feet.

The map must be of sand and can't be read by ordinary light. It
must carry fire to the next tribal town, for renewal of spirit.

In the legend are instructions on the language of the land, how it
was we forgot to acknowledge the gift, as if we were not in it or of it.

Take note of the proliferation of supermarkets and malls, the
altars of money. They best describe the detour from grace.

Keep track of the errors of our forgetfulness; the fog steals our
children while we sleep.

Flowers of rage spring up in the depression. Monsters are born
there of nuclear anger.

Trees of ashes wave good-bye to good-bye and the map appears to disappear.

We no longer know the names of the birds here, how to speak to them by their personal names.

Once we knew everything in this lush promise.

What I am telling you is real and is printed in a warning on the map. Our forgetfulness stalks us, walks the earth behind us, leaving a trail of paper diapers, needles, and wasted blood.

An imperfect map will have to do, little one.

The place of entry is the sea of your mother's blood, your father's small death as he longs to know himself in another.

There is no exit.

The map can be interpreted through the wall of the intestine—a spiral on the road of knowledge.

You will travel through the membrane of death, smell cooking from the encampment where our relatives make a feast of fresh deer meat and corn soup, in the Milky Way.

They have never left us; we abandoned them for science.

And when you take your next breath as we enter the fifth world there will be no *X*, no guidebook with words you can carry.

You will have to navigate by your mother's voice, renew the song she is singing.

Fresh courage glimmers from planets.

And lights the map printed with the blood of history, a map you will have to know by your intention, by the language of suns.

When you emerge note the tracks of the monster slayers where they entered the cities of artificial light and killed what was killing us.

You will see red cliffs. They are the heart, contain the ladder.

A white deer will greet you when the last human climbs from the destruction.

Remember the hole of shame marking the act of abandoning our tribal grounds.

We were never perfect.

Yet, the journey we make together is perfect on this earth who was once a star and made the same mistakes as humans.

We might make them again, she said.

Crucial to finding the way is this: there is no beginning or end.

You must make your own map.

THE END

*Pol Pot, infamous leader of the Khmer Rouge, responsible
for the killing of thousands, died peacefully in his sleep
April 15, 1998. His body was burned on a stack of old
tires, tended to by a few exhausted soldiers. In the midst of
the burning the fist of the corpse saluted.*

The dark was thicker than dark. I was a stranger there. It was a room
of ten thousand strangers, in a city of millions more.

The park across the street was heavy with new leaves
with an unbearable sensual drift

I had been sleeping for a few hours, and the room was thick with time
and ash. I wasn't dead though I was traveling

through the dark. The lower gods pounded the pipes for my
attention, the bed swayed with the impact of unseen

energy. No one saw it. No one saw anything
because it was dark and in the middle of the night and it was just

a hotel room, one of millions of hotel rooms all over
the world, filled with strangers looking for refuge,

sleep, for sex or love. We were a blur of distinctions,
made a fragrance like a glut of flowers or piss on concrete.

Every detail mattered
utterly, especially in the dark, when I began traveling.

And I was alone though the myth of the lonely stranger is a lie
by those who think they own everything even the earth

and the entrails and breath of the earth. This was the end.
It was Cambodia or some place like it, and the sun

was coming up, barely over the green in the restless shiver of
a million singing birds. Humans were wrapping

a body for burial. It stank of formaldehyde. It was a failed clay
thing, disheveled and ordinary. They rolled it

into a box and dragged it to a stack of trash. Why have I come here
I asked the dark, whose voice is the roar of history as it travels

with the thoughts of humans who have made the monster.
The fire was lit

fed with a wicker chair, a walking cane, and several busted
tires to make it hot. What I had

feared in the dark was betrayal, so I found myself there
in the power of wreckage. There was no pause

in the fighting. The killer's charred fist pointed toward the sky,
gave an order though no one heard it

for the crackle and groan of grease. The fire was dark
in its brightness and could be seen by anyone

on the journey, the black smoke a dragon in the sky.
This was not the end.

I was attracted by a city, by a park heavy with new leaves,
by a particular flower burning in the dark.

I was not a stranger there.

EMERGENCE

It's midsummer night. The light is skinny;
a thin skirt of desire skims the earth.
Dogs bark at the musk of other dogs
and the urge to go wild.
I am lingering at the edge
of a broken heart, striking relentlessly
against the flint of hard will.
It's coming apart.
And everyone knows it.
So do squash erupting in flowers
the color of the sun.
So does the momentum of grace
gathering allies
in the partying mob.
The heart knows everything.
I remember when there was no urge
to cut the land or each other into pieces,
when we knew how to think
in beautiful.
There is no world like the one surfacing.
I can smell it as I pace in my square room,
the neighbor's television
entering my house by waves of sound
makes me think about buying
a new car, another kind of cigarette
when I don't need another car

and I don't smoke cigarettes.
A human mind is small when thinking
of small things.
It is large when embracing the maker
of walking, thinking, and flying.
If I can locate the sense beyond desire,
I will not eat or drink
until I stagger into the earth
with grief.
I will locate the point of dawning
and awaken
with the longest day in the world.

SONGS FROM THE HOUSE OF DEATH, OR HOW TO MAKE IT THROUGH TO THE END OF A RELATIONSHIP

for Donald Hall

1.

From the house of death there is rain.
From rain is flood and flowers.
And flowers emerge through the ruins
of those who left behind
stores of corn and dishes,
turquoise and bruises
from the passion
of fierce love.

2.

I run my tongue over the skeleton
jutting from my jaw. I taste
the grit of heartbreak.

3.

The procession of spirits
who walk out of their bodies
is ongoing. Just as the procession
of those who have loved us
will go about their business

of making a new house
with someone else who smells
like the dust of a strange country.

4.

The weight of rain is unbearable to the sky
eventually. Just as desire will
burn a hole through the sky
and fall to earth.

5.

I was surprised by the sweet embrace
of the perfume of desert flowers after the rain
though after all these seasons
I shouldn't be surprised.

6.

All cities will be built and then destroyed.
We built too near the house of the gods of lightning,
too close to the edge of a century.
What could I expect,
my bittersweet.

7.

Even death who is the chief of everything
on this earth (all undertakings, all matters of human
form) will wash his hands, stop to rest under
the cottonwood before taking you from me
on the back of his horse.

8.

Nothing I can sing
will bring you back.
Not the songs of a hundred horses running
until they become wind
Not the personal song of the rain
who makes love to the earth.

9.

I will never forget you. Your nakedness
haunts me in the dawn when I cannot distinguish your
flushed brown skin from the burning horizon, or my hands.
The smell of chaos lingers in the clothes
you left behind. I leave you
there.

THE PATH TO THE MILKY WAY LEADS THROUGH LOS ANGELES

There are strangers above me, below me, and all around me and
we are all strange in this place of recent invention.

This city named for angels appears naked and stripped of anything
resembling the shaking of turtle shells, the songs of human voices
on a summer night outside Okmulgee.

Yet, it's perpetually summer here, and beautiful. The shimmer of gods
 is easier to perceive at sunrise or dusk,

when those who remember us here in the illusion of the marketplace
turn toward the changing of the sun and say our names.

We matter to somebody,
We must matter to the strange god who imagines us as we revolve
together in the dark sky on the path to the Milky Way.

We can't easily see that starry road from the perspective of the crossing
of boulevards, can't hear it in the whine of civilization or taste the
minerals of planets in hamburgers.

But we can buy a map here of the stars' homes, dial a tone for
dangerous love, choose from several brands of water or a hiss of oxygen
for gentle rejuvenation.

Everyone knows you can't buy love but you can still sell your soul for
less than a song to a stranger who will sell it to someone else for a profit
until you're owned by a company of strangers
in the city of the strange and getting stranger.

I'd rather understand how to sing from a crow
who was never good at singing or much of anything
but finding gold in the trash of humans.

So what are we doing here I ask the crow parading on the ledge of
falling that hangs over this precarious city?

Crow just laughs and says *wait, wait and see* and I am waiting
and not seeing anything, not just yet.

But like crow I collect the shine of anything beautiful I can find.

THE POWER OF NEVER

Never is the most powerful word in the English language, or perhaps any language. It's magic. Everytime I have made an emphatic pronouncement invoking the word *never,* whatever follows that I don't want to happen happens. Never has made a fool of me many times. The first time I remember noticing the powerful effect of this word I was a student at Indian school. My best friend, Belinda Gonzalez, and I were filling out our schedules for spring semester. She was Blackfeet, a voice major from Yakima, Washington. I was a painting major and checking out times for painting and drawing courses. She suggested I sign up for drama class with her. I said no, I will never get on a stage. Despite my initial protest I did sign up for drama class and soon was performing in one of the first all-native drama and dance troupes in the country. Never is that powerful!

And it doesn't matter when the statement is made, never makes its cruel spin as it hunts down a dreaded fate. It must be quite attractive in the epistemological world, a being with dark, luminous eyes, the physique of a cat. You will get on a stage, or in this case, you will move to Los Angeles at some point on your journey because you have just foolishly stated to a circle of friends that Los Angeles is the last place in the world you would live, you would never live there because it's smoggy, too much traffic, too many strangers and besides it is going to fall off into the ocean after one too many earthquakes, or one too many stupid movies.

So I moved to Los Angeles, into the heart of the beast, just off Hollywood and Wilcox to an apartment complex harboring a myriad of fools like me, some who probably made the same statement regarding the possibility of moving to Los Angeles, using that same word, *never*. Needless to say I was in shock as a new arrivee, from a quiet adobe condo near a bird sanctuary in Albuquerque where the daily music of life was the song of the sun moving across the sky, doves swinging on the telephone wires and other birds who considered the Rio Grande river valley a spa for their personal renewal.

I spoke with the crows before leaving for Los Angeles. They were the resident storytellers whose strident and insistent voices added the necessary dissonance for color. They had cousins in California, and gave me names and addresses, told me to look them up. They warned me, too, what they had heard about attitude there. And they were right. Attitude was thick, hung from the would-be's and has-beens and think-they-ares, so thick that I figured it was the major source of the smog.

And then there were the beautiful days when the perfume of flowers was everything and there appeared to be nothing else in the world, not the violence, the winos breaking bottles in the alley, the Spice Girls going up Hollywood Boulevard on a double-decker bus with low-flying helicopters accompanying them. The crows' cousins kept me company in that sometimes lonely and strange place as they paced the ledges of the crumbling buildings in my neighborhood.

One of the crows lived two apartments down from me. We lived on the third floor. He introduced himself to me shortly after I moved in when we met one day in the hallway. He gallantly took off his silk hat and bowed, said, "My name is R——, we take care of each other here." His slick black hair was perfectly groomed, his clothes shiny with money. Heavy music came through his door, and he had a steady stream of company, a perpetual party. He was always polite though the crowd of buyers grew large and raucous. Last I heard he was evicted for selling drugs, this crow with manners and a taste for the fine things in life.

I've considered using the power of never by trying for the opposite effect. For example: I will never win the lottery, or there will never be peace in this world. It won't work. It never will.

HOLD UP

for Greg Sarris

We were the twins, given birth to by a mother who loved the talk of gods.
She slept with the sun in the sky to have us—just when this world was ending.

And in that shifting time there was much danger, isn't that when these
    things tend
to happen? Giants are born and we could be swallowed by the monster.

That day we fled the changing of the worlds, we ran with tender blessings
into the streets, carried sharpened arrows and the promise of a father

who was a stranger. He could have been a musician, or a cowboy
but our mother pointed to the sun, and we burned brightly in our skins.

We went to school, worked jobs at the factory, and learned to buy everything
we needed. We forgot the smell and warning of the monster, and the reason

for the journey. The sun zigzagged across the land to watch us, made
a nimbic web that embraced us. Most humans breathed and died

without knowing they breathed planets. It's easy to get sidetracked and difficult
to see farther than the skin houses we walk this earth in.

Humans were created by mistake.
Someone laughed and we came crawling out.

146

That was the beginning of the drama,
we were hooked then.
What a wild dilemma, how to make it to the stars
on a highway slick with fear.

One night we stared at the glittering dark for clues.
For anything to sing, to shine—convinced someone had forgotten us.

In the whirlpool of the city the monster found us, walking in the glamour
without our arrows. It was two young boys who could have been our brothers,

they held us up, said they would kill us, as if we were no longer human,
or close to eagle. The payoff easy money, an itch for power. The moon

said nothing to them, neither did the creatures matter, or the flowers
who have a heart they share among themselves. We wanted to kill

the monster so it would not destroy the earth and take it with them,
or erase the dreams of humans in the ordinary world.

We gave them all our money in the whirling wake of violence,
the sun gleaming in our eyes made them walk the other way.

They wanted love, like we did, but did not know how to say it.

Humans were created by mistake.
Someone laughed and we came crawling out.
That was the beginning of the drama,

we were hooked then.
What a wild dilemma, how to make it to the stars
on a highway slick with fear.

The spirit of the story could smell the danger, climbed
down the clouds because things had gone too far.

It breathed in life from all directions. Included
the running boys in the beautiful pattern.

We followed.

RETURNING FROM THE ENEMY

for my father

1.

It's time to begin. I know it and have dreaded the knot of memory as it unwinds in my gut.

Behind me the river is steady and laps the jetty. Winds purr through the grass.

The wake of history is a dragline behind me. I am linked to my father, my son, my daughter. We are relatives of deep water.

Even the ghost crab disappearing into white gravel cannot escape the weight. The clacking of his joints makes a staccato against the danger.

Even a friend beside me in this perilous part of the journey stumbles on the slick of knowledge.

And the enemy who pressed guns to our heads to force us to Oklahoma still walks in the mind of the people.

But I hear relatives' voices in the wind as we gather for the reckoning. I carry fire in my hands to the edge of the water.

And continue to believe we will make it through the bloodstream to the ceremony for returning from the enemy.

2.

In the flickering mirror of time all events quiver in layers.

Each tree, each trigger of grass,

each small and large wave of water will reveal the raw story.

We climb and keep climbing, our children

wrapped in smallpox blankets to keep

them warm. Spider shows us how to weave

a sticky pattern from the muddy curses of our enemy

to get us safely to the Milky Way.

We had to leave our homes behind us,

just as we were left behind by progress.

We do not want your version of progress.

There are other versions, says Spider who does not consider making webs to sell to the highest bidder

but keeps weaving and thinking

and including us in the story.

3.

Vertigo is a terrible mode of travel.

It returns you perpetually to the funnel of terror.

I want it to stop and am furious that fear has found me here,

in the sun where people are laughing, doing ordinary things.

I want to be ordinary, I mean, with no worry that my house will be

burned behind me, that my grandchildren will become the enemy.

Here is the gravel singing under my feet, there are gulls

weaving the sky with horizon, alligators watch from the waters.

I walk with my friend to have lunch on the pier. I panic.

I want to know that I am worthy of all this sky,

the earth, this place to breathe.

I peer out from the house I have constructed from the hole in my heart,

I have returned to the homelands beloved by my people

who were marched to the west

by the authority of a piece of paper.

I keep warm by the fire carried through cruelty.

4.

Before speech I took language into the soft parts of my body. This was before I could fully digest meaning. It turned into bones, other hard parts:

I have held before me the god of fear. My heart is my house. A whirlwind is blowing it down.

I have bowed my head to those who would disrespect me. My neck appears to be broken in half by shame. I have lost my country.

I have handed my power over to my enemies. My shoulders bear each act of forgetfulness.

I have abandoned my children to the laws of dictators who called themselves priests, preachers, and the purveyors of law. My feet are scarred from the steps taken in the direction of freedom.

I have forgotten the reason, forgive me. I have forgotten my name in the language I was born to, forgive me.

5.

The enemy immigrated to a land he claimed for his God.

He named himself as the arbitrator of deity in any form.

He beat his Indian children

The law of the gods I claim state:

When entering another country do not claim ownership.

It's important to address the souls there kindly, with respect.

And ask permission.

I am asking you to leave the country of my body, my mind, if you have anything other than honorable intentions,

6.

When the enemy went after my father he spared no weapon
because he wanted, he said, my father's soul.

But it was the land he was after—this beautiful land of harbor
and sweet grass of palm tree and oak, of black earth, of red—

And we know that this earth cannot be owned by dictator or
church, by corporation or maker or signer of paper.

He took the land and moved all his relatives in. And when other immigrants
arrived from other lands he denied them what he had wanted for himself,

Though he wanted them for his customers.

The enemy made a circle of piss to claim us.

He cut everything down to make his cities and factories and

burned the forest to plant his fields. The wound so deep

it can be seen far above this blue-green planet, far above us.

You cannot destroy a soul though you may destroy a planet.

You cannot destroy a song though you can make a people forgetful.

A soul can appear to be destroyed, and a song can disappear for a
few generations only to reemerge from the cracks of sadness.

7.

Spirits who watch over us are summoned to the point of impact, to any major collision to which they are assigned.

Did they walk with us through the rivers, the swamps, though we could not see them there at the edge of our heartbreak?

Where are you? my father asked the dark waters as he walked through the rest of his life without us. He said this to her, the daughter of the watermonster not to us.

8.

We need a drink of water first, we tell the waitress who staples
brown paper to the table at the seafood restaurant in these lands
responsible for the delicate architecture of the marrow in my bones.

Backwards I fly, from Oklahoma, Arkansas, Mississippi, and
Alabama by plane, by the thread of a song shimmering in the sky.

By pure blood luck.

And suddenly I can see him over there, at the edge of the world,
the swamp of sea grass and ghost crab, fed by the river of history.
He's there, my father walking the brim, looking for her.

When a storm thunders miles out into the seas, the water in my
blood is storming.

Oh, water trembling with light, if I think of you the enemy disap-
pears into the deep.

9.

We sip our cool drinks in the world that is either flat or round,
depending on the point of view.

Consider the world is neither flat nor round.

Think again. Think, says water, as it makes a house for my father.

Think, says fire as it reconstructs the nearest star.

Between them is a field of meaning in which there is no word for *shame*.

There is incredible depth to every grain of sand, to every nuance
of creature, every gesture in the known and unknown universe.

Matter has converse weight in antimatter.

Destruction and creation in the shell of a little house were father
and daughter.

I try to appear as the savvy traveler, look smooth and inconspicuous
in this new knowledge.

No matter, I said lightly, more to myself than to anyone. We will
make it through this, past the edge of the wound.

10.

I sweat. It's hot in this lush palace of earth and water.

We talk as if we were travelers anywhere in the colonized world,
alert to tragedy and comedy,

We want to know if it's possible to separate and come back together,
as the river licking the dock merges with the sea a few blocks away.

Long-legged birds negotiate the shore for food.

I am not as graceful as these souls.

I am vulnerable to your beauty, the fronds of sea grass tangling the wound.

I am invisible, and there is an emergency rising from the mud.

11.

You are flushed from seawater and talking. Your style is radiant, and
dignity is your hair falling exactly to your shoulders, your brown fingers
have no doubt as to the ability to have what they want and need.

Your parents were gods who provided for you at any cost.

When you talk you weave a history sparkling bright with promise: a
friend swimming the Mississippi with a bottle of wine in his teeth to catch
up to the laughing crew, sunning nude in Provincetown, a friend you
should have married and it would have lasted forever, the friend's father
who mentored you and burned with the same flame that consumes you.

They all loved you without fail, without asking the question of
    your worthiness.

Your world is round and appears to gleam with perfection.

12.

I cling to your stories with my teeth, though I appear graceful, the winds of the water making my hair lift joyfully.

If I make your stories my life I will look bright in the new world.

I hold onto my paper plate stained with fried fish so it will not litter the river;

I hold onto my glass so I will not drown.

My eyes still blink with the force of the enemy's heels as he took down my father then headed for me.

I am trying to understand why the only story I can recall is drinking beer as a child on the beach of a man-made lake in Oklahoma.

I forget diving off the cliff into the water.

No one knows how deep or how shallow.

I feel nothing, hear nothing.

It doesn't matter.

Nothing matters.

13.

I say nothing because my story appears to be about loss and failure.

I say nothing because I believed the story of the superiority of the enemy, with all his structures, his money.

I say nothing as a skiff of American tourists unloads at the dock with trailing, whining children.

I say nothing because they appear to have inherited the earth.

I do not like this space of nothingness.

It is not the nothingness of wisdom.

It is the nothingness of nothingness, stirring up the water until no one can see.

14.

Our paths make luminous threads in the web of gravel and water.

The shimmer varies according to emotional tenor,

to the ability to make songs out of the debris of destruction

as we climb from the watery gut to the stars.

Just ask the ghost crab who turns to stare as he walks sideways

through the kingdom of suffering.

He shrugs then disappears into the beautiful world.

THE CEREMONY

All of my life I have entered into the ceremony from this door, toward the
    east into red and yellow leaves.

It has always felt lonely though there were always messengers, like the
    praying mantis on my door

when I opened it this morning. Or the smell of pancakes when there were
    no pancakes, coffee when there was no coffee.

I walked through the house we had built together from scraps of earth and
    tenderness, through the aftermath of loving too hard.

You were showering to get ready for war; I was sticky from late storms of
    grief and went to look for poetry.

Each particle of event stutters with electricity, binds itself to coherence.
    Like the trees turning their heads

to watch the human participants in these tough winds turning to go, as they
    continue to send roots for water making a language for beauty

out of any means possible though they are dying. Everyone is dying. I am I
    am, deliberately and slowly of this failure to correctly

to observe the ceremony of letting go ghosts of destruction. I walk carefully
    through the garden, through the hallway of sobbing and laughter,

the kitchen of bread and meat, the bedroom of desires and can see no
   ghosts though they will take the shape of objects of ordinary living.

There is no poetry where there are no mistakes, said the next messenger. I
   am a human being, I said.

THIS IS MY HEART

This is my heart. It is a good heart.
Bones and a membrane of mist and fire
are the woven cover.
When we make love in the flower world
my heart is close enough to sing
to yours in a language that has no use
for clumsy human words.

My head, is a good head, but it is a hard head
and it whirrs inside with a swarm of worries.
What is the source of this singing, it asks
and if there is a source why can't I see it
right here, right now
as real as these hands hammering
the world together
with nails and sinew?

This is my soul. It is a good soul.
It tells me, "Come here forgetful one."
And we sit together with lilt of small winds
who rattle the scrub oak.
We cook a little something
to eat, then a sip of something
sweet, for memory.

This is my song. It is a good song.
It walked forever the border of fire and water

climbed ribs of desire to my lips to sing to you.
Its new wings quiver with vulnerability.
Come lie next to me, says my heart.
Put your head here.
It is a good thing, says my soul.

PROTOCOL

I do not know your language though I hear the breaking of waves
through the vowels.

It is blue and if I am to follow protocol I will introduce myself
through my mother and hers until you know the liquid mass of ancestors
and in that you might know that I did not find myself
here on your island by some coincidence.

When you walk toward me from the ocean you are cobalt
and the people whose chants have constructed the intimate
canyons of your bones can be glimpsed suddenly as water clings
to your skin, your hair. I can hear the singing.

My spirit flew across the country of blue water
on a path made of a song that shifts the molecular structure
of rain clouds whenever it is recalled.

Migrations form a network of sense
that mimics neuron patterns
in the wave of dolphins, water, and humans.

When the Mvskoke emerged from that misty original place
we were led by four young winds, and a star who took the form
of talking fire. After we set up camp some of us went to look for water.

I found it years later, near the scarlet volcano just as it was predicted,
when companies of white men have fooled themselves and the
sleeping ones into thinking they've bought the world.

My family still has the iron cooking pot that was traded to us
when treaties were forced with blood. Those who signed were killed.
Now I have a gas range and there is no end to the war.

When I arrive from the sky after traveling through clouds
and the afterburn of jets I will consider the gift
of those who kept walking though their feet were bloodied
with cold and distance, as their houses and beloved lands
were burned behind them.

I will consider the tyranny of false rulers and how though they
appear to dominate your island they are small and brittle and will break.

When we meet at the gates of power you honor me with pikake and maile
and a chant that allows me to paddle with you into the waters
so I will not be known as a stranger.

I offer you coral and tobacco and a song that will make us vulnerable
to the shimmer of the heart, allow us to walk the roots
with our peoples through any adversity to sunrise.

This is how I know myself.
This is how I know who you are.

MORNING SONG

The red dawn now is rearranging the earth
Thought by thought
Beauty by beauty
Each sunrise a link in the ladder
Thought by thought
Beauty by beauty
The ladder the backbone
Of shimmering deity
Thought by thought
Beauty by beauty
Child stirring in the web of your mother
Do not be afraid
Old man turning to walk through the door
Do not be afraid

From

New Poems
1999–2001

IN PRAISE OF EARTH

We kept on dancing last summer though the dancing had been called subversive.
We weren't alone at the end of this particular world and knew
it wouldn't be the last world, though wars
had broken out on all sides.

We kept on dancing and with us were the insects who had gathered at the grounds
in the grasses and the trees. And with us were the stars and
a few lone planets who had been friends
with the earth for generations.

With us were the spirits who wished to honor this beloved earth in any beautiful
manner. And with us at dawn was the Sun who took the lead
and then we broke for camp, for stickball
and breakfast.

We all needed praise made of the heart's tattoo as it inspired our feet or wings,
someone to admire us despite our tendency to war, to terrible
stumbles. So does the red cliff who is the heart
broken to the sky.

So do the stones who were the first to speak when we arrived. So does the flaming
mountain who harbors the guardian spirits who refuse to abandon
us. And this Earth keeps faithfully to her journey, carrying us
around the Sun,

All of us in our rags and riches, our rages and promises, small talk and suffering.
As we go to the store to buy our food and forget to plant, sing so

that we will be nourished in turn. As we walk out
into the dawn,

With our lists of desires that her gifts will fulfill, as she turns our tears
into rivers of sweet water, we spiral between dusking and
dawn, wake up and sleep in this lush palace of creation,
rooted by blood, dreams, and history.

We are linked by leaf, fin, and root. When we climb through the sky to each
new day our thoughts are clouds shifting weather within us.
When we step out of our minds into ceremonial
language we are humbled and amazed,

at the sacrifice. Those who forget become the people of stone who guard
the entrance to remembering. And the Earth keeps up her
dancing and she is neither perfect nor exactly in time.
She is one of us.

And she loves the dance for what it is. So does the Sun who calls the Earth
beloved. And praises her with light.

LETTER (WITH SONGLINE) TO THE BREATHMAKER

We yearn for you, oh Maker of Breath,
for it appears that you have abandoned us
in the shadow world to the lower gods
who trick us with the gleam of casinos,
while two fat butler birds swing on the plumeria.

The mist of remembering saturates the flowers,
my newspaper is damp with humidity.

We want to see you, Breathmaker, not just the evidence
of you. We can see the sheen of your breath in
the circle of dancers in their ribbons and turtles,
the singers resplendent with carved shells and
cowboy boots as they move with the fire that speaks to you.

The shimmer of the sun polishes the mist necklace adorning
the mountain but what makes the source of your breathing?

We are sick with the stories of those political parties
who would destroy our tribal nations.
They have a reason, they say, and there is reason
behind any massacre, whether it be on our lands
or on paper. These lands have been turned
into gunneries, these papers into roads for war.

The winds surfing through the Ko'olau Mountains
refresh us with the thoughts of young forming stars.

Oh Maker of Breath if you are the shine woven
through all things, from the plumeria blossoms
clustered on the tree of knowledge to the destroyers
in the bay across the water then where does justice begin
and cruelty end in this talking and thinking world?

A butterfly with wings like lungs carries pollen in the direction of the sun.
We will search for you urgently everywhere.

I AM NOT READY TO DIE YET

My death peers at the world through a plumeria tree
And the tree looks out over the neighbor's house to the Pacific
And the blue water god commands this part of the world
Without question, rules from the kingdom of secrets
And tremendous fishes. I was once given to the water.
My ashes will return there,
But I am not ready to die yet
Nor am I ready to leave the room
In which we made love last night.

This morning I carry the desire to live, inside my thigh
It pulses there: a banyan, a mynah bird, or a young impatient wind
Until I am ready to fly again, over the pungent flowers
Over the sawing and drilling workmen making a mess
In the yard next door, over water
And the memory of your shoulders
In candlelight.

It is endless, this map of eternity, like a watermonster
Who swallows everything whole including the bones
And all the terrible words and how it blooms
With delectable mangoes, bananas
With the most faithful of planets,
But I am not ready to die yet.

And when it happens, as it certainly will, the lights
Will go on in the city and the city will go on shining

At the edge of the water—it is endless, this map
And the waves of longing from the kingdom of suffering
Will linger in the room in which we made love last night—
When I am ready to die I will know it,
As surely as I know your gaze
As we undressed close to the gods in that room.

There will be flowers, there are always flowers,
And a fine blessing rain will fall through the net of the clouds
Bearing offerings to the stones, to all who linger
Here—It will be a day like any other.
Someone will be hammering
Someone frying fish
The workmen will go home
To eat poi, pork, and rice.

NAMING

for Vanessa, Toshi, Krista, and Tamarin

I call my sisters to dress for the stomp dance
As all the little creatures hum and sing
in the thick grass around the grounds.
Lightning bugs are tiny stars
dancing in the river of dusk.
Our stomachs are full of meat and fry bread
and the talk of aunts and uncles.
Beautiful fire at the center of the dance
and the dusk has been lit.
We lace up our turtle shells so we
can dance into the circle.
And in this spirit world is the grocery
store over the hill, and all the houses,
the river, the sky, and the highway.
We have been here forever
say our mother, our father.
And this is the name we call ourselves
I tell my sisters,
this name that gives our legs the music
to shake the shells—
a name that is unspeakable
by those who disrespect us
—a name with power to thread us through
the dark to dawn
and leads us faithfully to the stars.

FAITH

In Krakow
The spires of churches
Fit the skyline exactly
They have been rendered
By prayers of the faithful
Who built the church on their knees
My faith is a limp thing
In this distant city
Strung together
With cold rains
And clouds
Crows mark the border
Between despair
And joy
They are
Poets of noise—
Needed, because the question
Is too large to fit
One city, one church,
Or one country
I am far away from the answer
Wherever I go
This dark month
Of the overthrow
The sleep of idiots

Would be sweet
But disasterous
I might miss
The feet of god
Disguised as trees.

EQUINOX

I must keep from breaking into the story by force
for if I do I will find myself with a war club in my hand
and the smoke of grief staggering toward the sun,
your nation dead beside you.

I keep walking away though it has been an eternity
and from each drop of blood
springs up sons and daughters, trees,
a mountain of sorrows, of songs.

I tell you this from the dusk of a small city in the north
not far from the birthplace of cars and industry.
Geese are returning to mate and crocuses have
broken through the frozen earth.

Soon they will come for me and I will make my stand
before the jury of destiny. Yes, I will answer in the clatter
of the new world, I have broken my addiction to war
and desire. Yes, I will reply, I have buried the dead

and made songs of the blood, the marrow.

AH, AH

for Lurline McGregor

Ah, ah cries the crow arching toward the heavy sky over the marina.
Lands on the crown of the palm tree.

Ah, ah slaps the urgent cove of ocean swimming through the slips.
We carry canoes to the edge of the salt.

Ah, ah groans the crew with the weight, the winds cutting skin.
We claim our seats. Pelicans perch in the draft for fish.

Ah, ah beats our lungs and we are racing into the waves.
Though there are worlds below us and above us, we are straight ahead.

Ah, ah tattoos the engines of your plane against the sky—away from these
    waters.
Each paddle stroke follows the curve from reach to loss.

Ah, ah calls the sun from a fishing boat with a pale, yellow sail. We fly by
on our return, over the net of eternity thrown out for stars.

Ah, ah scrapes the hull of my soul. Ah, ah.

MORNING PRAYERS

I have missed the guardian spirit
of the Sangre de Cristos,
those mountains
against which I destroyed myself
every morning I was sick
with loving and fighting
in those small years.
In that season I looked up
to a blue conception of faith
a notion of the sacred in
the elegant border of cedar trees
becoming mountain and sky.

This is how we were born into the world:
Sky fell in love with earth, wore turquoise,
cantered in on a black horse.
Earth dressed herself fragrantly,
with regard for the aesthetics of holy romance.
Their love decorated the mountains with sunrise,
weaved valleys delicate with the edging of sunset.

This morning I look toward the east
and I am lonely for those mountains
though I've said good-bye to the girl
with her urgent prayers for redemption.

I used to believe in a vision
that would save the people
carry us all to the top of the mountain
during the flood
of human destruction.

I know nothing anymore
as I place my feet into the next world
except this:
the nothingness
is vast and stunning,
brims with details
of steaming, dark coffee
ashes of campfires
the bells on yaks or sheep
sirens careening through a deluge
of humans
or the dead carried through fire,
through the mist of baking sweet
bread and breathing.

This is how we will leave this world:
on horses of sunrise and sunset
from the shadow of the mountains
who witnessed every battle
every small struggle.

THE EVERLASTING

for Ingrid Washinawatok

This is not poetry. Poetry cannot exist here
in the field where they killed her.
There are no flowers though there appear to be flowers.
There is a splatter of blood, there is a pool of blood
there is a raining of blood.
When the soldiers were done with the killing they wiped her
off their hands with gritty rags and a slap of water.
They left the bodies in that field
to the flying, stinging creatures, to damp butterflies of sadness
and pain, to the eyes of the everlasting who
catalogues the cruelties of humans
from one nation to another
from one ragged scar
to another.

And the soldiers went on with their living, ate
their dinner that night around a small fire,
their arsenal stacked against a tree.
They relished cervezas, sucked pig bones.
They called their mothers, their sons, their daughters
from their cell phones.
They remembered birthdays, mourned their dying,
sang love songs for their wives and mistresses waiting
for them in the city, in the countryside.

"We walked 30 kilometers today
through this damned unforgiving country.
We had orders. And we fulfilled them," they said.
And they were given their rations, and money
to send home while they fought this war
that was not officially a war.

Nor were these officially soldiers and any allusion to killing
was just an allusion to killing.
And according to official documents
the sun is not the sun.
There is no gunpowder
for addition and subtraction.
No not, no nothing.
And the moon is not the moon
watching everything
that happens in the dark.

Nor was I dreaming when I saw this in a dream:

I was out of my mind. I would rather be out of mind
in this field of betrayal and useless killing.
A hummingbird who poised urgently
at the screen door
was out of my mind.
It traveled on pure nerve and singing
from the thread of the spirit
of all that makes beauty

before turning into a breaking sky
into a river of blood.
And back to the trap of reason
of argument. I must
be out of my mind.

No killing. Did you ever see her walk toward you?
That sad love song you are singing to the moon
moved her to dance, close, so close to the stars
to the man she loved. And here is a dress
that still smells of her sweetness
like purple flowers raining.
Her moccasins of deerskin cured by smoke, so she will know
the way to maples and rivers,
to a nation that is out of its mind
with grief for losing her.

Nothing seems to change—said the message
unwound by the hummingbird.
But there was a light by which I could
see the soldiers through the wings.
It's dawn. They are coughing with cigarettes,
drinking coffee, picking their teeth of meat.
A half day over the mountain are travelers
they will kill because it has become easy to kill.
Because there is a reason to kill.
And reason kills reason.

The wound in the earth where they took her
is being tended by rain
and flowers.
Oil companies will soon dig crude there,
with their machinery, their money,
and instant cities of missionaries and soldiers
will beget a countryside
of children of missionaries and soldiers.

This is the story of the new world, revealed
in the songline gleaming in the dark. It is thin, breakable.

It can be broken into the smallest chips of bone and tears.
It can be put back together with sunrise and flint.

AND IF I AWAKEN IN LOS ANGELES

I will find a crazy boy teetering there
on the sidewalk against morning traffic,
too far gone to even ask for a quarter.
I will hear his mother call for him,
her spirit confused by the taste
of sadness,
and though she searches for him
everywhere,
she will never find him here.

And if I awaken in Los Angeles
I will hear the lost beloved one
sing Billie Holiday in my ear—
she lives in a parallel universe,
is kind to rats and does
no harm to anyone.

And if I awaken in Los Angeles I will know
that I am not the only dreamer.
I will appear in the vision of a dove
who perches on the balcony
of the apartment.
In his translation I am the human with a store
of birdseed. He is the sun.
I am a fruitful planet.

And if I awaken in Los Angeles
I will not have to get up and say my prayers
to the east, and look out over the city of millions,
past the heads of palm trees, through foggy breezes—
because I will be a prayer as I perform the rituals
of being a human.
There will
be no difference
between
near and far.

This morning I have too much to do to awaken.
I say my prayers, feed the birds,
then head to the refrigerator and forget.

IT'S RAINING IN HONOLULU

There is a small mist at the brow of the mountain,

each leaf of flower, of taro, tree and bush shivers with ecstasy.

And the rain songs of all the flowering ones who have called for the rain

can be found there, flourishing beneath the currents of singing.

Rain opens us, like flowers, or earth that has been thirsty for more than a season.

We stop all of our talking, quit thinking, or blowing sax to drink the mystery.

We listen to the breathing beneath our breathing.

This is how the rain became rain, how we became human.

The wetness saturates everything, including the perpetrators of the second
   overthrow.

We will plant songs where there were curses.

RUSHING THE PALI

There's not enough time,
no puka to squeeze through
the head, then the shoulder
then the rest of it
a perfect creation
with hands, feet, and
a mystical heart.
It's too late.
I've promised a ride
to hula, and then
I am to paddle
to Kewalo
and back in sprint time
that is after the cleaners
and a few phone
calls to figure out how
to remove
mildew from synthetics.
There is holy woven
through all life
if that is so then even in the rush
can be found
mythic roots for example how
this island was formed
from desire and fire
from the bottom of the sea

and how we came to be
here, next to the flowers
teased by winds
who travel freely back and forth
from the other side.
I am attracted
by the songs of the holy
curling indigo,
sea turtles alongside the canoe
or a mist of elegant consciousness
floating above the clatter
of annoyance.
There was dawn and the color
of ashes just before the sun
when the spirits of dancers before us
joined and the earth moved
lightly because she was
moved.
Singing is behind it.
We can sing ourselves
to the store or eternity as surely
as we were born into
this world naked and smeared
with blood and fight.
No time to keep putting it off
these thoughts of the holy
first one petal, and then
another, like sunrise

over the Pacific
until there is a perfect human.
And then rain over the Pali
as we slow for a stop,
and then the traffic starts
all over again.

WHEN THE WORLD AS WE KNEW IT ENDED

We were dreaming on an occupied island at the farthest edge
of a trembling nation when it went down.

Two towers rose up from the east island of commerce and touched
the sky. Men walked on the moon. Oil was sucked dry
by two brothers. Then it went down. Swallowed
by a fire dragon, by oil and fear.
Eaten whole.

It was coming.

We had been watching since the eve of the missionaries in their
long and solemn clothes, to see what would happen.

We saw it
from the kitchen window over the sink
as we made coffee, cooked rice and
potatoes, enough for an army.

We saw it all, as we changed diapers and fed
the babies. We saw it,
through the branches
of the knowledgeable tree
through the snags of stars, through
the sun and storms from our knees
as we bathed and washed
the floors.

The conference of the birds warned us, as they flew over
destroyers in the harbor, parked there since the first takeover.
It was by their song and talk we knew when to rise
when to look out the window
to the commotion going on—
the magnetic field thrown off by grief.

We heard it.
The racket in every corner of the world. As
the hunger for war rose up in those who would steal to be president
to be king or emperor, to own the trees, stones, and everything
else that moved about the earth, inside the earth
and above it.

We knew it was coming, tasted the winds who gathered intelligence
from each leaf and flower, from every mountain, sea
and desert, from every prayer and song all over this tiny universe
floating in the skies of infinite
being.

And then it was over, this world we had grown to love
for its sweet grasses, for the many-colored horses
and fishes, for the shimmering possibilities
while dreaming.

But then there were the seeds to plant and the babies
who needed milk and comforting, and someone
picked up a guitar or ukulele from the rubble

and began to sing about the light flutter
the kick beneath the skin of the earth
we felt there, beneath us

a warm animal
a song being born between the legs of her,
a poem.

FROM *THE LAST SONG*

Watching Crow, Looking South . . .

The *Manzano Mountains* are just south of Albuquerque and formed a crucial part of my imagination during the genesis of these poems. I particularly remember cool fall mornings, stories of Isleta deer hunting told by my Isleta friends as we ate and participated during feast days and other family events. Deer songs thread the mountainside interweaving the paths of deer and can be heard especially in those magic golden and scarlet-leafed fall days.

Although this is the first poem in the collection, it was not the first poem I ever wrote. The first poem was of a singer/dancer telling the story of the animal he was hunting and as he tells and sings the story he becomes the animal. The poem was inspired by watching such an event.

for a hopi silversmith

For *Phil Navasaya*, a Hopi artist whose jewelry is characterized by a swift elegance and familiarity with rain clouds and prevailing winds. His family sustained me in my early years in Albuquerque when I was an undergraduate student at the University of New Mexico. Phil's mother Rita always treated me like a relative. Phil's fiercely intelligent brother coached me in math my first year at the University of New Mexico, and his sister Anna is one of my oldest friends of that circle (along with Carmen Foghorn and Marley Shebala).

San Juan Pueblo and South Dakota . . .

I first presented this poem at the first native women's literature conference in the mid-seventies in Tsaile, Arizona, on the Navajo reservation at what was then known as Navajo Community College. The poem was briefly interpreted by an audience member as a condemnation of Siouxs. Later we had a good laugh about it as this wasn't the intention. We were all in it together in those years during our search for justice, for a means to justice and a relief for injustice. Okie's, the legendary bar at the corner of University and Central in Albuquerque, was where many of us landed after those heavy meetings of discussions in which we had to face the devastation of history and what we were going to do about it. At Okie's a pitcher of beer could relieve the intense pressure of being human in a time and place of much inhumanity.

Barbara Wells-Faucon was a brilliant and cutting observer of the comedy and tragedy of being Indian in the mid-seventies.

The *Sandias* are the mountains that define Albuquerque. They mark the point east, which is the direction of beginnings, and the road toward Oklahoma.

he told me his name was sitting bull

Sitting Bull or *Tatanka Yotanka,* Hunkpapa Sioux was one of the principal chiefs who negotiated the Fort Laramie Treaty of 1868, a treaty that forced the United States to abandon several forts and respect the Lakota's claim to the sacred Black Hills, or Paha Sapa. He came to power during an era of great turmoil and immense changes for his people and all native people on this continent. He was born in 1830 into a time in which the Sioux lived relatively free of European contact. By his death, in 1890, that world was nearly unrecognizable.

As a very young man Sitting Bull had killed a buffalo, counted coup on an enemy, and was initated into the Strong Heart Warrior Society. Soon after he naturally assumed leadership and was held in great respect throughout his whole life. He joined with other Sioux bands to defeat Custer in 1876 at Little Bighorn. Sitting Bull's dreams foreshadowed the defeat of Custer. During a June 1876 Sundance, after thirty-six hours of dancing, Sitting Bull had a vision of the U.S. Army soldiers without ears falling into a Sioux village, upside down. The lack of ears signified ignorance of the truth, and the upside down positioning indicated their death. Gold was soon discovered in the Black Hills and the land was soon overrun by squatters digging for gold. In the 1870s he and a few hundred of his people took refuge in Canada. There he had visitors from around the world. In 1881 he returned to the United States and surrendered. He was taken to the Standing Rock Agency where he ridiculed efforts to sell Indian land. Although he adopted farming and sent his children to reservation schools he said, "I would rather die Indian than live a white man." He endorsed the vision of the Paiute prophet Wevoka, a vision of restoration for native peoples. Sitting Bull was killed a few days before the massacre of ghost dancers at Wounded Knee as forty-three tribal police tried to arrest him (reference from *The Encyclopedia of Native American Biography*, Bruce E. Johansen and Donald A. Grinde Jr., Da Capo Press, New York, 1998).

Anadarko is a major town in southwestern Oklahoma. It marks the border of the Great Plains and many Indian nations of the southern Plains converge here, including the Kiowa, Commanche, Southern Cheyenne, and Apache.

Tahlequah is the capital of the Cherokee Nation west of the Mississippi located in northeastern Oklahoma. The Illinois River runs through it.

3 A.M.

Old Oraibi is a Hopi village on *Third Mesa* and is known as the most traditional village of the Hopi nation. The village has successfully resisted installation of electricity and the establishment of outside religions.

Acoma is a pueblo village located west of Albuquerque (or rather Albuquerque is located east of Acoma), a distance of about sixty miles.

Are You Still There?

Laguna is a Keresan pueblo reservation west of Albuquerque.

Mesita is one of many Laguna villages. Other villages include Seama, Paraje, Paguate, Encinal, New York, New Laguna, Old Laguna, and Philadelphia. The Rio Puerco runs through Laguna and is often the center of much activity as it has been for centuries. Many of the stories and poems of Leslie Silko take place here. Laguna is on the way to Acoma if you are coming from Albuquerque.

Conversations Between Here and Home

This was written before the institution of shelters for battered women. In those earlier years we made our own shelters, took each other in, nursed each other, laughed and cried together. One of the makeshift shelters we named "Heartbreak Hotel."

NOTE—All of the poems here appeared in the subsequent publication, *What Moon Drove Me to This?*

FROM *WHAT MOON DROVE ME TO THIS?*

Four Horse Songs

I was made aware of horse songs by Simon Ortiz, who sings a song/poem about a man trying to make it home through the winter of his life. It was called either "Beauty Roanhorse" or "Buny Roanhorse." Simon says in a correspondence of August 23, 2001: "I haven't thought about it in a while. And I don't remember all the words either. . . . You see when I first heard the story of a man with that name I heard the name as Beauty Roanhorse. So when the song came about (1976 or 77 or 78?), when I began to hum and sing it, it was 'Beauty Roanhorse.' Beauty Roanhorse, Beauty Roanhorse, I would say. But then I had heard wrong because I heard the correct pronunciation by the one who told me the story. 'Buny' or 'Beaunie.' Or however it might be spelled. Maybe like 'Bewnie.' The *u* sound like in *new* or *puny*."

When I hear Navajo horse songs I see the beautiful multicolored lands of Dinetah and feel the ground shaking with the running of horses. I see a road of relatives from home all the way back to Monahwee and his black horse running the red roads of the southeast, through the lush homelands, feel the thrill of flying hard and fast on the back of a horse. Horses teach me about the power of vulnerability. They make swift connections between wind and blood.

These four horse songs don't have the same quality of exhilaration and praise as the horse songs that inspire them. They take place in those black holes between despair and home. This area is treacherous and crisscrossed by bootleggers and railroad tracks and is characterized by the pain of failure and loss. Border towns perch here and depend on the business of the native people and on tourists brought in with the lure of native culture, but return the gift with terrible human rights abuses.

There Was a Dance, Sweetheart

Carmen Foghorn was a student at the University of New Mexico and a member of our politically active Indian student organization, the Kiva Club.

Central Avenue is the main street defining the center of Albuquerque and follows the historic Route 66.

Mount Taylor is one of the sacred mountains of the Navajo, and the mountain informing the shape of Acoma culture.

Crows appear nearly everywhere. They are tricksters of a sort and very human in their crowness. I see them as the chorus, outlining and commenting on the unfolding drama of this world.

Crossing the Border

From an indigenous point of view, the border between Canada and the United States doesn't exist. It is an imaginary line imposed by invader nations with governing laws that are arbitrary. Many tribal nations are slashed by the border. Among those affected in the north are the Mohawk and Anishnabe, and Yaqui and Tohono O'odham in the south. Crossing the border is always hazardous for Indians. We are singled out and searched, detained, and questioned.

Barney Bush is a Shawnee poet and writer. When I was in graduate school in Iowa City he was living and teaching in Milwaukee. I was lonely for Indian country as I was one of only seven Indian students at the University of Iowa. He heard about a Delaware powwow in *Moravian Town*—"just the other side of Detroit"—and called to ask, "Do you want me to pick you up on the way?" "Yes," I said. "I'm dying here." Of course, Iowa City is not technically "on the way" to the other side of Detroit, rather several hundred miles "out of the way." And I was not technically "dying," just lonely for Indians.

Richard Jack was Barney's Menominee sidekick.

Someone Talking

The *Man of Words speaks like the cricket* refers to an image by N. Scott Momaday in his collection, *The Way to Rainy Mountain:* "Once I looked at the moon and caught sight of a strange thing. A cricket had perched upon the handrail, only a few inches away from me. My line of vision was such that the creature filled the moon like a fossil. It had gone there, I thought, to live and die, for there, of all places, was its small definition made whole and eternal. A warm wind rose up and purled like the longing within me" (from *The Way to Rainy Mountain,* University of New Mexico Press, Albuquerque, 1969, p. 12).

Noni Daylight is a fictional character who appeared in these early poems. First, the name Noni Daylight came forth as a cover for anonymity, then she invented herself as a full-fledged woman with a history and walked out of my poems. The last time I saw her was in the late seventies, when she appeared in a poem by Barney Bush. I never saw her again.

The poem "Someone Talking" has been revised. Among the revisions was the substitution of whiskey for the particular of Old Crow. There were too many proper nouns in the poem, a weakness of my earlier poems. I didn't want to delete it as the original reference to Old Crow was a tribute to my friend Geary Hobson, a fellow writer and professor of mine at the University of New Mexico. I wish the tribute to remain, however, though the poem isn't directly about him.

Fire

This poem is also a revised version. The original included too many proper nouns for such a small poem.

FROM *SHE HAD SOME HORSES*

Call It Fear

Goodluck is a common Navajo surname.

In the early 1970s the forty-nines in Albuquerque—which were the late-night reveries of Indians missing home and needing to sing to remember in the midst of cities and change—took place at the Juan

Tabo campground area in the foothills of the Sandias. The park service stopped them there, chained off the area so we moved to the Volcano Cliffs area of Albuquerque on the west side of town. This area is characterized by sweeping volcanic flows toward the Rio Grande. From this vantage point you can see the lights of Albuquerque, the heart of the mountains, everything.

Anchorage

Audre Lorde was a warrior-poet who inspired many in her intense, well-lived life as a black, lesbian, human rights artist. The first I saw of her poetry was the book *Coal* (first published by W. W. Norton, New York, 1976), which jumped out at me off a bookshelf in the student bookstore in Iowa City. These were poems honoring her blackness and the poems provoked a shift within my own work. I had been struggling to find myself against the slant of European thought and form. "Anchorage" was inspired by her poem "Litany for Survival" from her collection, *The Black Unicorn* (first published by W. W. Norton, New York, 1978). I first heard her read the poem in Minneapolis in the very early eighties. That poem I consider the heart of her body of work. A spirit resides there. It feeds and continues to feed poetry.

On March 27, 1964, the second most powerful earthquake in recorded history devastated Anchorage. It registered 9.2 on the Richter scale and lasted approximately 4 to 6 minutes. More than a hundred people died, most of them from the tsunami that followed with huge waves of terrible power on the Pacific coast from Alaska all the way to Crescent City, California. The death toll could have been much worse had there been a denser population. It was the houses of the rich, I was told when I first visited Anchorage in April of 1984 as a guest of an Alaska native arts program, that tumbled into the ocean during that shaking of the earth.

Nora Dauenhauer is a fine Tlinget poet and translator of Tlinget literature. She now lives outside Juneau with her collaborator and husband, Richard Dauenhauer. Their first collaboration was a major inspiration. *Because We Cherish You—Sealaska Elders Speak to the Future* (Sealaska Heritage Foundation Press, Juneau, Alaska, 1981) was transcribed, translated, and edited by Nora and Richard. Nora Dauenhauer's most recent book of poetry is *Life Woven with Song* (University of Arizona Press, Tucson, 2000).

Athabascan speakers encompass an extensive group from the Chipewyan, Kutchin, Carrier, and Sarsi peoples (in Canada), to the Tlinget (in Alaska), the Chasta-Costa (in Oregon), and the Hoopa (in California), to the Navajo (in New Mexico, Arizona, and Utah) and the Apache (in New Mexico, Arizona, Utah, Oklahoma, and Texas).

In the late seventies or early eighties I visited Juneau and Anchorage, Alaska, as a visiting poet in one of the many national programs for taking poetry into the prisons. In Anchorage I was advanced $300 in cash of my travel monies to pay a deposit to Rent-A-Wreck for a refurbished police car, the only car I could rent because I didn't own a credit card. I always tried to park it inconspicuously—so that none of the inmates would see the car and think I was an informer or police, though no one could probably see me, the car, or much of the outside at all.

In every prison and jail in which I was locked with inmates for the few hours of my workshops, stories and poems unraveled and with them tears, shame, desperation, and hope. Most of the prisoners were native and constituted a disproportionate number of the total prison population. Next were the black prisoners, and then the poor white men who'd come up north to work on the pipeline. They were in mostly for small crimes involving drugs and money. There I learned intimately the power of spoken and written word, how steel bars, fear, and oppression can be relieved by songs, poetry, and stories.

Nearly every inmate could recite literature from memory. Some recited their own poems, poems they memorized in school or their own poems kept tucked in their scarred hearts.

I'll always remember Henry in the 6th Avenue jail in Anchorage. Every one of his outrageous stories was true, stories of impossible tests, escapes. Despite the bars he was still on the adventure of life and his spirit was buoyant, it shined. The last time I saw him he was called out to clean up the blood mess of his friend who had just attempted suicide. He bowed as he left us, pushing the mop and bucket the guard shoved to him. Henry's heart was larger than that northern city and was what probably landed him in jail. He'd broken the law to help out a friend.

For Alva Benson . . .

Alva Benson was a fellow student at the University of New Mexico and a member of the politically active Indian student organization, the Kiva Club. She was deeply engaged in the major issues of those times, like the destruction of Black Mesa for coal, the mining of uranium, and the random and sadistic killings of native peoples in Navajoland and all over the country. I admired, too, the way she walked that difficult line of being half Navajo, half "biligaana" in a time when there were few breeds in the Navajo Nation. Graceful, I can still see her entering a meeting carrying her daughter, and then later with her daughter by her side as she passed out fliers and announcements for various political actions. Her life was taken suddenly by a freak accident that many say was not an accident, for there are no such events as accidents in our lives. We still miss her.

The *Indian Hospital* is usually a clinic or several clinics attached to a hosptial administered by the Indian Health Service, a branch of the Public Health Service (PHS). These hospitals are often the only health care facility for native people and serve many with severely limited funds and personnel.

Mount Saint Helens is a young volcano in the Cascade Range in the State of Washington, and was once known as the "Fuji of America" because of her resemblence to the famous Japanese volcano. On May 18, 1980, she erupted for a continuous nine hours and devastated more than 150 square miles of rest and recreation area, killing countless animals and leaving sixty people dead or missing. (USGS, Science for a Changing World, Cascades Volcano Observatory, Vancouver, WA, CVO Website—Mount Saint Helens Volcano, WA)

The eruption had been predicted in Mvskoke and other tribal prophecies as the marker of an era that would be characterized by destruction and loss if the inhabitants of this continent didn't change the current of thinking, and remember to honor the gift of life.

Gloria Bird comments in the introduction of *Reinventing the Enemy's Language, Contemporary Native Women's Literature* (W. W. Norton, New York, 1997, p. 24): "my aunt once, when we were looking at what was left of Mount Saint Helens, commented in English, 'Poor thing.' Later, I realized that she spoke of the mountain as a person. In our stories . . . our relationship to the mountains as characters . . . is one of human-to-human. What was contained in her simple comment on Mount Saint Helens, Loowit, was sympathy and concern for the well-being of another human being—none of which she has to explain."

Loowit is a northwest tribal name for Mount Saint Helens.

Meridel LeSueur (1900–1996) was the inspiring novelist and poet of the American 1930s. She was one of the very few writers of the thirties to focus on women, women who lost jobs, faced starvation, who struggled for survival. She wrote from a place of great female power. Birth and fecundity of the earth and all life were her major themes. I met her in Albuquerque at a gathering and she took me in, became a mentor, and stood by me during my struggles to become a poet. After the eruption of Mount Saint Helens she told me about the meaning of *harmonic motion* while we were driving in a car between Albuquerque and Santa Fe. She characterized it as the tremor of the earth as she gives birth, speaking of the context of the volcanic action as a labor contraction, giving birth to another world.

The Woman Hanging from the Thirteenth Floor Window

There is no *east side of Chicago*.

A popular style of jeans in the late 1970s and early '80s were *Levi's 501's*.

One of the U.S. programs to attempt to disappear native people was a program called *Relocation*. The goal was the disappearance of Indian people, the logic being that if Indian families moved to the cities for jobs, to live, that they would become acculturated, would forget their "Indianness." The federal government pushed for relocation of Indians from the late 1940s through the 1960s. Under relocation programs in those years, many Indians looking for jobs and housing moved into cities such as Chicago, Dallas-Forth Worth, Denver, San Francisco, Los Angeles, or Oklahoma City. Don Fixico has written the first ethnohistory of modern urban Indians titled, *The Urban Indian Experience in America* (University of New Mexico Press, Albuquerque, 2000).

White Bear

This poem was inspired by a series of prophecies told by Phillip Deer, an esteemed Mvskoke tribal member. In one of the predictions, I recall the image of a white bear moving down from the north. There was much speculation as to what the white bear symbol meant. Some thought the white bear represented the countries of Russia or China taking over North America. Others believed the image was directly connected to the blowing of Mount Saint Helens and the white ash that covered the Pacific Northwest from the fury of the explosion.

New Orleans

Conti Street, Royal, and *Decatur* are streets in the French Quarter section of New Orleans.

The *French Market* is an open market and has been in operation since New Orleans began as a city in 1718.

Hernando DeSoto was the first European contact by the Mvskoke Creek tribe. He landed on the western coast of Florida in 1539, bringing with him wishes and dreams for riches, an attitude of entitlement (backed up with an army in armor, mounted on horses), and numerous diseases for which the Creeks had no immunity.

Usually it is just the Cherokee whose forced migration from east to west is recognized as *"The Trail of Tears,"* but there were many tribes forced west, including the Mvskoke Creeks. The removal took place in stages. Some groups were taken by a southern route through New Orleans, brought up the Mississippi River on steamboats to the Arkansas River. The *Monmouth* was one of the contracted boats. On July 31, 1836, it was being piloted recklessly by a drunk crew when it collided with the *Trenton,* another steamboat. The *Monmouth* broke up and sank, killing over three hundred of the migrating Creeks. Many of those who survived were badly scalded by hot water.

She Had Some Horses

This poem was inspired by Simon Ortiz's poem/song for his daughter Rainy, "There Are Horses Everywhere." (Simon Ortiz's most recent book of poetry is *After and Before the Lightning,* from the University of Arizona Press, 1994, part of the Sun Tracks Series.)

*Creek Stomp Dance song*s are traditional Mvskoke songs that are a call and response form with rhythm (and meaning) provided by turtle shell rattles tied to the women dancers' legs. Dancers move counterclockwise around the fire.

I Give You Back

This poem was inspired by Audre Lorde's poem, "A Litany for Survival," from *The Black Unicorn* (W. W. Norton, 1978).

FROM *SECRETS FROM THE CENTER OF THE WORLD*

If You Look with the Mind of the Swirling Earth

Shiprock or *Naat'aani Neez* is a large Navajo community in the northwest part of New Mexico. It is marked by a huge rock that appears to look like a ship. *Naat-aanii* means boss, chief, or leader. *Neez* means tall.

It Is an Honor

The book and many of my poems are influenced by Navajo philosophy and literature. This is an excerpt of the *Navajo Night Chant* song. N. Scott Momaday, the Kiowa writer and artist, published it in his Pulitzer Prize–winning novel, *House Made of Dawn* (the most recent printing is the HarperCollins, New York, 1999 edition):

Tsegihi.

House made of dawn,
House made of evening light,
House made of dark cloud,
House made of male rain,
House made of dark mist,
House made of female rain,
House made of pollen,
House made of grasshoppers,

Dark cloud is at the door.
The trail out of its dark cloud.
The zigzag lightning stands high upon it.
Male deity!
Your offering I make.
I have prepared a smoke for you.
Restore my feet for me.
Restore my legs for me.
Restore my body for me.
Restore my mind for me.
Restore my voice for me.
This very day take out your spell for me.
Your spell moves from me.
You have taken it away for me;
Far off it has gone.
Happily I recover.
Happily my interior becomes cool.
Happily I go forth.
My interior feeling cool, may I walk.
No longer sore, may I walk.
Impervious to pain, may I walk.
With lively feelings may I walk.
As it used to be long ago, may I walk.
Happily may I walk.
Happily, with abundant dark clouds, may I walk.
Happily, with abundant showers, may I walk.
Happily, with abundant plants, may I walk.
Happily may I walk.
Being as it used to be long ago, may I walk.
May it be beautiful before me,
May it be beautiful behind me,
May it be beautiful below me,
Maybe it be beautiful above me,
Maybe it be beautiful all around me.
In beauty it is finished.

Grace

I attended graduate school in Iowa at the Iowa Writers' Workshop during two of the worst winters of the century. The world slowed down with the freeze and the lack of sunlight was nearly devestating to this sun lover. I felt abandoned by the giver of life. Everything froze: the sky, exhaust from vehicles, my ability to write or dream and I didn't always handle it well. I took myself and my complaints too seriously and let the dark take me down. In those bleak moments Darlene Wind always reminded me to laugh, and we had plenty to laugh about given history and how we ended up in Iowa City at Iva's doorstep, trying to make it in this world. Iva Roy took us in, showed us around that country that belonged to her people, the Meskwaki, or the Fox. My children found family with hers, ran through the cornfields that are no longer there. She took us home to the Meskwaki Settlement where the people have maintained integrity of culture in the midst of cornfields and a European mind field. The excellent poet Ray Young Bear whose most recent book, *The Rock Island Hiking Club* (University of Iowa Press, 2001), is from the Settlement.

I got out of Iowa as soon as I got my degree and headed back to New Mexico and the sun, stopping as always in Oklahoma. It wasn't until 1994 when I returned to speak and perform for the Iowa Summer Writers' Program that I went back to the city that had tested me, with cold, with loneliness, with self-doubt. When I landed at the Cedar Rapids Airport I called home to check my messages. There was an urgent message from Darlene. I hadn't heard from Darlene in a long while, too long. The message was short, sorrowful. Iva Roy had died suddenly and her body had been sent back to Iowa and would I meet her there for Iva's wake, the burial? Strange that in all the several thousand days since I left Iowa I return on the one day, the day of Iva's final return. But no coincidence. There is no such thing as coincidence. There is a meaning to the pattern no matter how convoluted.

I prepared myself and drove out to the Settlement to pay my

respects to Iva's family, then drove to the funeral home in Tama for another farewell. Iva's body had been dressed in traditional clothes for her journey. I'd only seen her in her modest dress of T-shirt and jeans, or her shawl at powwows. Any money always went for rent and food and getting the children what they needed, and then their children, not for new clothes. I spoke to her, giving her my thank-yous for all the kindnesses, the good times, and then prayed for her journey to the place in which she would not have to struggle so hard for her life. I know I will see her again.

James Welch is a major Blackfeet writer and poet from Montana. His first book of poems, *Riding the Earthboy 40* (Harper & Row, New York, 1971), and his first novel, *Winter in the Blood* (Harper & Row, New York, 1974), inspired me early in my writing career. My first meeting with Jim was in Amsterdam in 1980 for the One World Poetry Festival. It was an amazing event, with poets in from everywhere in the world including Jamaica and Africa. Most inspiring was to meet Okot p'Bitek from Uganda whose lyric poem, *Song of Lawino* (East Africa Publishing House, Nairobi, Kenya, 1969), is a world classic. He died shortly after that festival. Watching Linton Kwesi Johnson, the dub poet from Jamaica perform in the Milkweg made me think of rhythm in poetry differently. Rhythm starts from the inside, from the heart of the human, the planet, the solar system, the universe. It's coherence; it's the core.

Jim and I hooked up. We were interviewed together and I admit we were very irreverent and did not act the part of the Indians the press had romanticized. Jim did not have hair down his back or feathers and beads, but looked rather scholarly and sheepish, and I was dressed like any twenty-something poet on the fringes of the world. We escaped. It was Jim's birthday. We had dinner with Allen Ginsberg and his entourage, then walked one end of Amsterdam to another, from the red-light district to the lobby of the hotel from which we had to call a taxi because no one dared to pick us up on the street in that nearly dawn hour. I've always enjoyed Jim's hangback wit, his appreciation of beauty and symmetry of humans and stories.

I wrote the first draft on the back of an envelope while flying back from a writing conference in Grand Forks, North Dakota, where Jim and

I had read together. We'd all gotten a little crazy on mescal the night before, convinced the sponsor to swallow the worm, claimed it was an old Blackfeet/Creek tradition and we would be offended if he refused the worm. He did so heartily. This poem is dedicated to Jim because as I flew over Iowa the whole state was white with snow and I recalled the time I did in Iowa and the winters of Jim's world and how a laconic humor makes the slide a little easier.

Coyote and *Rabbit* are trickster figures, that is, the prototypes for humans. Bob Thomas, a wise and witty Cherokee professor in American Indian Studies at the University of Arizona, told me once over biscuits that Rabbit is neither male nor female, rather an androgynous figure who walks the edge.

Leech Lake is a reservation in Minnesota of the Leech Lake Band of Ojibwe.

Deer Dancer

The *Buffalo Calf Woman* appeared to the Lakota at a time when they needed to know how to live. John Fire Lame Deer says in *Seeker of Visions, The Life of a Sioux Medicine Man* (an autobiography cowritten with Richard Erdoes, Simon & Schuster, New York, 1972) that in those times "They knew nothing. The Buffalo Woman put her sacred mind into their minds." She appeared to the Lakota in both a human form, as a beautiful woman, and as a buffalo. She brought to them the sacred pipe, corn, wasna (or pemmican), wild turnip and taught the people many things, showed them the right way to live. When she left she said she would return every generation cycle. The birth of the white buffalo in Janesville, Wisconsin, on August 20, 1994, is understood by many as the return as promised of White Buffalo Woman. Arvol Looking Horse, the caretaker of the White Buffalo Calf Woman pipe in this generation, said as he prepared for a ceremony at the Janesville farm shortly after the birth of the calf, "The prophesies are being fulfilled. . . . We are starting to see a coming together of people going back to their natural ways" (from "Looking Horse Family Keepers of Original Lakota Sacred Pipe," by Neal White, *Beloit Daily News,* September 13, 1994).

There are many stories of the face of Jesus appearing in a tortilla.

The first I knew occurred in a small town in northern New Mexico, near Chacon where my friend, the poet Leo Romero, was born. The face of Jesus appeared on a *burned tortilla* meant for breakfast. It was considered a miracle and many people from all over New Mexico, even Mexico, made pilgrimages to see the Christ image in the tortilla. Many miracle cures were attributed to the sight.

In the introduction of Carolyn Dunn and Carol Comfort's anthology *Through the Eye of the Deer* (Aunt Lute Books, San Francisco, California, 1999), the editors remind us that the traditional Mvskoke Deer Woman "is the spirit we are warned about as children, the spirit that bewitches those who are suseptible to her sexual favors and who can be enticed away from family and clan into misuse of sexual energy" (p. xi).

The way it was told to me it was on the night of a blizzard that a mysterious young Indian woman in a red dress suddenly appeared in the Milwaukee Indian bar. When the popular country western tune sung by Kenny Rogers came on she stood on a table and peeled off her clothes, dancing with memory to the sad ballad of a man bemoaning the fact that his beloved *Lucille* left him *with four hungry children and crops in the field*. She had the sudden attention of the tatters of men playing pool who could not believe the vision. Then, went the story that as the song neared the end many of them ran over to the jukebox and fed it with quarters, punching in C-12 LUCILLE. *Lucille* over and over again all night, until way past closing time. The song is still playing in that bar way up north. I always wondered what happened to her, after her dance on the sticky, worn table in the bar, a dance driven by heartache on a night when the whole town had closed for the storm and only fools went out in it. Did she make it to where she was going? Did someone lend a hand or was she ambushed by other desperate ones after the dance? Did she go home? I've kept a place in my heart for her. There are tall stands of pine trees near a clear, deep lake. It is early in the morning and she is safe.

For Anna Mae Pictou Aquash . . .

In February 1976, an unidentified body of a young woman was found on the Pine Ridge Reservation in South Dakota. The official autopsy attributed death to exposure and alcohol. The FBI agent present at the

autopsy ordered her hands severed and sent to Washington for fingerprint-
ing. John Trudell, one of the leaders of the American Indian Movement,
rightly called this mutilation an act of war. Her unnamed body was buried.
When Anna Mae Pictou Aquash, a young Micmac woman who was an
active American Indian Movement member, was discovered missing by her
friends and relatives, a second autopsy was demanded. It was then discov-
ered she had been killed by a bullet fired at close range to the back of her
head. She had not died of exposure and there was no alcohol in her blood.
Her killer or killers have yet to be identified.

Bird

Charlie Parker was also known as *Bird* or *Yardbird*. *Yardbird* is
another word for chicken and Parker loved to eat chicken. *Bird* was for
Parker's tendency to fly, to run either in his life or on his horn. He revo-
lutionized jazz with harmonic possibilities and an amazing rhythmic syn-
tax. He *was* bebop, a movement of jazz characterized by dazzling
improvisation of complex harmonic and rhythmic idioms.

The *Catalinas* and *Rincons* are two of the mountain ranges that sur-
round Tucson, Arizona.

The Real Revolution Is Love

Managua is the capital of Nicaragua.

Yerbabuenas are drinks made with healthy portions each of rum,
fresh mint, sugar, and water. I first had one in Nicaragua around 1986
at the International Poetry Festival hosted by the liberation theologist
priest and poet Ernesto Cardinale.

Diane Burns is an Anishnabe poet from Wisconsin who lives in New
York City. Her first book of poetry *Riding the One-Eyed Ford* (Contact II
Publications, New York, 1981) is a classic of contemporary American
Indian poetry.

I saw a vision of a wild-haired Puerto Rican dressed all in black car-
rying a painted black suitcase with some kind of non sequitur splashed in
white ink across it. I thought: I am imagining things, imagining humans
and I was and I was not. It was Managua and we were all checking into

the festival, a poetry festival in Nicaragua. The vision was real and I met *Pedro* Pietri, a Puerto Rican–American poet from New York City. He appeared to be acting but he wasn't acting. The comic import of life was there in his large, compassionate eyes, in every gesture—all born from his heart. I immediately loved him, as did everyone: other poets, kids, dogs, the sun, the moon.

A few mornings later the poetry delegation scrambled to be up at dawn though we had partied most of the night. Our ride, a flatbed truck headed for the coffee plantation in Matagalpa, was waiting and we couldn't find Pedro, just his shoes. Of course, this led to all kinds of speculation and we reluctantly left without him. When we returned later that afternoon, there he was fresh and crisp from a shower, from lounging and making friends at the market with the locals. He told our dusty and exhausted crew what happened. In the early morning hours after the yerbabuena party he had fallen asleep on the couch of what he thought was our suite, the poets' suite. When he woke up the next morning he sat down at the table with the other guests—a delegation of visiting Russian diplomats stiffly having breakfast. He wondered where we were and why this strange group was suddenly there at our communal table. He sat with them, smiling as he drank his coffee and ate his bread. He didn't understand why they kept staring at him until he saw himself in the mirror later. His hair was straight up and he had forgotten to put on any clothes.

The poem "The Real Revolution Is Love" was revised after several musical performances with my first band, Joy Harjo and Poetic Justice.

Song for the Deer and Myself to Return On

Louis Oliver or Little Coon was born April 9, 1904, in Coweta, Creek Nation, Indian Territory, and was of the Raccoon Clan. He was also the oldest and most earnest student in a one-day workshop of Creek and Cherokee students I taught in the late seventies at the Flaming Rainbow University in Tahlequah, Oklahoma. After the class he approached me with a stack of poetry he had been writing on his own for years, poems dependent on European verse forms. My workshop was the first time he realized that he could abandon the strict metrics and patterns of European forms and take up more organic forms, forms that fit his Muscogean subject matter. Shortly thereafter he met native poets: Carroll Arnett, Cherokee; Barney Bush, Shawnee; Lance Henson, Cheyenne; and Joseph Bruchac, Abnaki, and began writing the wise and witty poetry that would comprise his published work. *The Horned Snake* was published in 1982 (Cross-Cultural Communications, Merick, New York) when he was seventy-eight years old. His last book was *Chasers of the Sun: Creek Indian Thoughts* (Greenfield Review Press, Greenfield Center, New York, 1991).

Santa Fe

The *DeVargas Hotel* has been reborn as the Hotel St. Francis and sits at the corner of Don Gaspar and Water Streets in Santa Fe.

There are sacred places on this earth, places that generate power, hold and even protect power. People are drawn to these places, including "power" companies that translate power into economic terms. Assisi is one of these places, the home of St. Francis. I was familiar with *St. Francis* because as a high school student at Indian school I often walked by the *St. Francis Cathedral* in Santa Fe and read the plaque under the statue of St. Francis. I learned that he is considered by Catholics as the patron saint of animals, that he lived between the years of 1182 and 1226, and was the cofounder of the Franciscan Order. He was born into a wealthy family but denounced his father's wealth in 1206. Francis then began to live as a hermit and lived a simple lifestyle, a lifestyle that included love and respect for all life. He composed a famous poem, "Canticle of Brother Sun," in which he praises the Sun and Moon and Stars as living beings, as well as Wind and Air. He saw love (God) in all living things, which was quite heretical in those days, even in these days.

The power of that love as it revealed itself in St. Francis is still in Assisi. I was stunned to feel it there when I visited in 1998. I didn't expect it. It is a palpable power, especially in the small chapel built by him and his followers, and in the fields and trees of the countryside. It is still there, transforming the world. That love blew me open. In Assisi was the first time I ever felt such love in a church. And it wasn't about the church at all, it came from the countryside on which the church was built, from the sun, the moon, the connection of all life including the plants and animals. This is my understanding of the meaning of power, of St. Francis.

Desire

This poem could not have been written without Wallace Stevens's "Thirteen Ways of Looking at a Blackbird" (from *Collected Poems*. Copyright ©1923 and renewed 1951 by Wallace Stevens. Alfred A. Knopf, Inc., New York).

The Book of Myths

The island of *Manhattan* was purchased by the Dutch from a delegation of hunters who were just passing through the area in pursuit of deer, for $24 worth of trade goods. They were not the lands' owners. The indigenous people at that time had no concept of ownership of land.

Nadema Agard, a Cherokee, Lakota, and Powhatan artist lives near Inwood Park, the site where the Dutch purchased the island. She was told by a very elderly Indian woman some twenty years ago that Indian people were still living in the park in the early twentieth century. Indians also had squatting rights in Central Park, before it became Central Park in 1859.

Hunter College is a liberal arts college on the Upper East Side of New York City. Audre Lorde had a presidentially appointed position there as a poet-in-residence in the 1980s.

Helen of Troy in Greek mythology was considered the most beautiful woman in the world in fifth century B.C. Greece. She was the daughter of the god Zeus and of Leda, wife of King Tyndareus of Sparta. Helen's beauty was the direct cause of the Trojan War.

Marilyn Monroe is an American goddess. The actress's blonde, pouting looks and accentuated figure became the standard of Euro-American female erotic power in the mid-twentieth century.

Transformations

Once in the very early eighties I stayed at the house of two friends in Santa Fe as I prepared for a solo journey around the United States.

Early one morning while I was up writing I saw a moving shadow in one of the bedrooms and got up to check it out. My friend was still sleeping in the half-light of early morning. Standing next to her was her other-self, a shadow self who was urgently trying to get the attention of the sleeping self. It made sense given the condition of her life as a woman caught between two lovers.

Eagle Poem

The *Salt River* or Rio Salado flows through Tempe, Arizona. Josiah Moore, an O'odam and Pima educator, leader, and friend, told me that the river was an historical gathering place for his people. He remembered when the banks were lined with cottonwoods. He remembered horses and wagons lined up along the river, enjoying the cool oasis. When he told me this in the early eighties the river had been dammed and was kept in Lake Roosevelt. What remained was a winding dusty ditch that became an angry river after the urgent rainstorms that arrived every rainy season. Now, I've heard, there is water again because the City of Tempe businesses wanted the water to flow again through the city.

FROM *THE WOMAN WHO FELL FROM THE SKY*

The Creation Story

There are many versions of the *creation story*. In one Mvskoke version the ground opened up and the people came out. The Wind Clan people were the first to emerge. Henry Marsey Harjo, my great-grandfather was of the Wind Clan; my great-grandmother Katie Monahwee of the Tiger Clan. Because clan association traditionally comes through the mother, my father's mother was the Tiger Clan. She passed this clan on to him, and I am associated with this clan.

The Woman Who Fell from the Sky

The inspiration for "The Woman Who Fell from the Sky" is a classic, an Iroquois creation story of the same name. A pregnant woman falls (or is pushed, depending on the version) through the hole beneath the Great Tree. She falls and falls until birds assist her, carry her to the back of the Sea Turtle. On Sea Turtle's back she grows roots and plants she has carried from the Sky World. This is the beginning of this world as we know it (www.crystalinks.com/iroquois.html).

There were many stories of children like Johnny who ran away from Indian *boarding school* and froze to death or lost their feet to the cold. Laura Tohe's award-winning collection of poems, *No Parole Today* (University of New Mexico Press, Albuquerque, 1999), addresses the Indian school experience.

I once traveled far above the earth for a different perspective. It is possible to travel this way without the complications of NASA. This beloved planet we call home was covered with an elastic web of light. I watched in awe as it shimmered, stretched, dimmed, and shined, shaped by the collective effort of all life within it. Dissonance attracted more dissonance. Harmony attracted harmony. I saw revolutions, droughts, famines, and the births of new nations. The most humble kindnesses made the brightest lights. Nothing was wasted.

The Flood

Embedded in Muscogee tribal memory is the tie snake or *estakwvnayv*, a large blue watersnake who can transform himself. He represents the power of the Lower World.

A Postcolonial Tale

This poem was rewritten to be performed. When the band was rehearsing it, a chorus was added and I rearranged the poem to go with a song form based on a northern style Plains powwow song.

The Myth of Blackbirds

Countless treks have been made and are still being made by Indian delegations to the capital of the "biligaana-white-man-wacichu-este-hvtke-haole," or Washington, D.C., to discuss business on a nation to nation basis.

Letter from the End of the Twentieth Century

The *Igbo* are a west African tribal people.

One of the world's largest airports is *O'Hare,* west of Chicago.

Tallahasee Grounds or *Tvlvhasse* is a ceremonial grounds of the upper Creeks, reestablished in Indian Territory.

Promise of Blue Horses

All time is simultaneous. It is layered and may appear in the shape of a coiled snake or in waves like the ocean. The inside is the outside.

The Place the Musician Became a Bear

I heard about *Jim Pepper* years before I ever met him during one of my trips to perform poetry in New York, and he invited me, a beginning sax player, to his apartment in Brooklyn. We listened to the sax gods of Ben Webster, Cannonball Adderly, and his other inspirations and influences, talked Oklahoma and home, and then he'd disappear for his fix, the subway beneath his apartment building shaking the world like a huge underground snake. He'd return with a smile and we'd keep listening. Deeper and deeper.

Jim was a fine jazz tenor and soprano jazz saxophonist and, at the urging of Don Cherry and other musicians with whom he played, had begun constructing a music that married the traditional elements of jazz with Muscogean and Plains tribal musics.

I've always believed us Creeks had something to do with the origin of jazz. It only makes sense. When the west Africans were forced here they were brought to the traditional lands of the Muscogee peoples and, of course, there were interactions between Africans and Muscogees.

So, it wasn't so strange for Jim to pick up a saxophone and find his way to jazz.

When he died I knew he had gone to the Milky Way and had left us his gift of music—I think of him at the ceremonial grounds when I see the fire climb, turn to stars.

Or when I walk the streets of New York City and hear the music of the subways.

Fishing

Night crawlers are earthworms used for fishing bait.

A few weeks before he died I wrote my friend the Muscogee poet,

Louis Oliver, a promise I would go fishing with him in Oklahoma that summer. Fishing to Louis was a holy communion. The struggle of the universe is exemplified in the sport. It's possible to find the right answer to every question with the right pole, the right place in the river.

As I mailed the letter I had a strange feeling the letter would never reach him. That cloud of illogic hovered over me for a few days. When I was informed of his death, I knew I had to keep that promise.

This is how I kept it.

Promise

The spring before my granddaughter Krista's birth I was a passenger on a plane approaching Tucson. We ran into storm clouds and were told to expect violent turbulence. I understood the rain clouds were there at the request of the earth, to bring rain. I requested mercy, that the plane be guided down gently. They gathered not long after for Krista's birth. I knew they were with us, blessing her.

The Dawn Appears with Butterflies

I was on my way to Tuba City, located in northern Arizona in the heartland of Hopi and Navajo country. I'd made plans to stop at Second Mesa in Hopiland to see some friends of mine whose daughter was going to take part in the Butterfly Dance, her first dance.

I stopped first at Rosanda's mother's house for exact directions, as I had been told. She told me to come in; she had some bad news. Rosanda's husband had died quite suddenly of a condition that had been in remission. Because he had so looked forward to his daughter's participation in the Butterfly Dance the family decided to go ahead with her part in it. They knew that he would be able to see her anyway, that his spirit was much like a butterfly.

The next few days unfolded with grief as well as laughter as the family prepared for the burial and release of this man who had lived respectfully. They told stories, fed visitors, they remembered him by sharing.

The afternoon before his burial Rosanda went to pick out the shirt in which to bury him. She brought a couple of them into the living room to show me.

"What do you think of this one?" she asked. "I bought this shirt for him three years ago. It's my favorite and he would never wear it."

We laughed, thinking of him wearing the shirt she loved, the shirt he refused to wear, through eternity.

I'm sure he laughed with us. That's the way he was.

FROM *A MAP TO THE NEXT WORLD*

Songline of Dawn

The original use of the word *songline* refers to the Australian Aboriginal concept of enforcing relationship to the land, to each other, to ancestors via the mapping of meaning with songs and narratives. Bruce Chatwin suggested in *The Songlines* (Penguin, New York, 1987) that the whole of Australia could be read as a musical score, where a musical phrase is like a map reference.

All has been sung into existence. Every sunrise is sung and makes a continuous dawning all over the world. I am connected to my daughters and son by thought, by heart just as they are connected to their children, and so on and so on. Eventually we all connect: humans, animals, plants, planets, universes, deity.

There is a small *wetlands* just off I-25 in Albuquerque, north of an exit just past I-40. It is a small pond of cattails and grasses not much larger than three or four junked cars. During my last visit there was reconstruction of that part of the highway and the wetlands may have been destroyed by the earthmovers. The morning sun always lingered there in fall and spring, in the company of migrating birds.

A Map to the Next World

In the months before the birth of my third granddaughter Desiray, a Navajo deity appeared to a blind woman who lived far away from the cities in a distant part of the reservation. This was an unusual occurrence, something unheard of in recent history. Such visits come about historically only in times of terrible stress, when the people have lost their way. The deity explained that the people were in danger, and that unless they kept up the traditions that made them particularly Navajo, a complex and beautiful system of prayer and thanksgiving, they would suffer the loss of what makes them powerful in this world.

After this visit many people made pilgrimages to the old woman's hogan to see the place the deity stood, to hear the story once again and talk about it with each other. We who heard the story in Albuquerque talked about it, pondered it as we watched the kids' basketball games, ate dinner together, or dressed for work. We considered the meaning and timing of the appearance of this shimmering one, and wondered how it will continue to mean in this world apparently driven into craziness by violence and greed.

The End

Perhaps there is a current called "the end" and we catch the wave of it by luck, karma, or some other means of logic. Each process has a cycle. The end is one part of the cycle and it recurs according to the spin. The night of the poem the end slithered through the unconciousness of the city. It appeared in the dark vaguely as a giant lizard, close to the Mvskoke description of a tie snake, a monster from the waters of the deep conscious. It whipped around, knocking dreamers into nightmares, dragging us through our fears at the deepest point of the night.

Why does evil exist? I ask the question we all continue to ask. And why does evil often sit in the chairs of rulers, presiding over history, over human and other lives they are charged to protect? We are the ones who give these people power. Andrew Jackson became president after receiving high war honors by the U.S. government. He was responsible for the killing of Mvskoke women and children who resisted being forced from their homelands.

Why is it leaders are chosen according to the ability to acquire power and money, not because of their outstanding gifts of service, compassion, and love for the community?

Destruction is the part of any process, like weeding, and we need to constantly hone ourselves to be made strong, not to rule and destroy but to continue toward a beautiful sense of meaning and order. There is an exact address of compassion and in this place even Pol Pot and Andrew Jackson will one day open their eyes. But it is sometimes difficult to translate this knowing into the here and now where men like Pol Pot and Andrew Jackson are honored for their acts and are perceived as powerful, and women raising children are not.

Songs from the House of Death . . .

I imagine someone walking through the ruins of my house, years later when I am gone and anyone who knew me and my family and nation is gone and there are only speculations as to what happened to us. The shells and shards of memory are searched for meaning. Did we flee from an enemy, or die of famine or floods? I think back to the ruins of a house in Chaco Canyon, Anasazi ruins near Crownpoint, New Mexico. The winds are cool and steady and through the years they have eroded the adobe. There is no protection from the sun and rain. Tourists quickly pass through ruins. The clouds, too, walk on. Everything keeps moving. Even me, moved by my thoughts through the house, through time. I converse with my own death, which is already leaving a track behind me, like the ruins of this house.

The Path to the Milky Way Leads Through Los Angeles

Okmulgee is the capital of the Creek Nation west of the Mississippi. It is said that my family once owned most of the town. And there's a story told me by my Aunt Lois Harjo who talked of the appearance of the first traffic light in town. She and her mother and sisters stood at the corner waiting for the signal to cross. When the light turned green they tentatively started across, then the light turned yellow. "My mother was so nervous," she said, "she turned around and slapped your grandmother." I think about this every time I drive through Okmulgee and pass by that traffic light that still dangles above the street. It is probably the original one.

The Power of Never

Our drama and dance troupe from the Institute of American Indian Arts toured the Pacific Northwest, including the theater under the Space Needle in June 1968. The show was called *Deep Roots, Tall Cedar*. It featured the plays of Monica Charles, Klallam playwright, and choreography by Rosalie Jones, Blackfeet. We were directed by Roland Meinholtz. He taught us all aspects of stagecraft and treated us as professionals. We responded in turn.

Hold Up

I follow my friend Greg from the truck up the sidewalk. I can smell the water of the Pacific in the air. Two young boys approach on the sidewalk. Greg greets the boys with familiar terms, as one would speak to young relatives on the road: "Hello brothers." Next I hear in response from a young male voice: "I am going to kill you." I step back in slow motion and cannot believe I am hearing this. A tree rustling with empathy blocks my view. I feel as if I am dreaming this until the second boy is suddenly holding a gun to my head and tells me to give him everything. Now they are no longer boys. They are harbingers of death, holding our lives in their childish, dangerous hands.

I imagine a karate kick, the gun flying up as the boy sprawls disabled on the ground and I turn to take on his partner, but I also know in my lizard brain that this could trigger a panic that could kill my friend and/or myself. I split into several tracks of awareness. I can hear the spin of the earth, literally. The urge to live surges through the trees, each blade of grass, each particular flower and leaf surrouding us.

My death is a huge thing, too large to argue with but I do comment that it is a little earlier than we agreed on. And death says nothing but nods its head. Also, I note to death, I do not want to die without honor, here on the streets of this city by the hands of children. I think of the twin monster slayer stories of the Navajo. Perhaps the monsters are disguised as these two baby thieves. Or maybe in their eyes we are the monsters, the ones who appear to have money because of the neighborhood they found us in. I think of my babies but I have to turn my heart the other way or I will dissolve into grief. Yet I know this is not the natural end of the story, not the way our linked destiny had it in mind, and still I know that everything can turn, unnaturally, sudden.

The boy with the gun at my head almost shoots me with his cheap gun because he is terrified. Strange to find a child in the face of a monster and I want to ask him, "Where is your father, your mother?" but that wise voice in me says, "Be quiet!"

Then the boy backs up, his gun pointed at my heart. I can hear Greg's voice in the dark, and see the boys backing off, their guns still aimed at us to keep us back. They turn to walk off into the twisted maw of the glittering city, counting our money, our possessions as bounty. Only then do I hear the pounding of my heart. Only then do I feel the tremble of Greg's life as we hold each other up.

Returning from the Enemy

"*Grandmother Spider* [my italics] appears in many forms in tribal narratives. She is woman as Creatrix, giver of life, guide, nurturer, and protector" (Carolyn Dunn and Carol Comfort, *Through the Eye of the Deer,* Aunt Lute Books, San Francisco, 1999, p. xiv).

The use of *smallpox infected blankets* was a form of chemical warfare employed to destroy native peoples in North America. The idea apparently came from Lord Amherst who in a letter of orders to Colonel Bouquet in July of 1763 said, "Could it not be contrived to send the Small Pox among those disaffected tribes of Indians? We must on this occasion use every stratagem in our power to reduce them." Bouquet replied that he would try and use infected blankets as a means of introducing the disease among the Indians, but was wary of the effects it would have on his own men. In his book, *The Conspiracy of Pontiac* (vol. 2, Bison Edition, The Library of America, New York, 1991, also edited by William P. Taylor), Francis Parkman also states that there is no evidence that Bouquet ever used the smallpox plan, although an epidemic raged among the Ohio Indians "a few months after" the above correspondance.

Ghost crabs live on sandy beaches of the Atlantic coast of North America and can be quite large. They are also very musical and are both percussionists and singers. A *ghost crab* came to give me a message in New Smyrna Beach outside a fish-and-chips place located between the beach and the river. The crab was quite wise and in one glance I saw the beginning and end of an era of emotional turmoil. I'll always remember his dignity as he turned and disappeared into the waving sea grass.

The Ceremony

My band was performing two shows a day a the Cultural Olympiad at the 1996 Olympics in Atlanta when the bomb exploded near the stage we had played on just a few hours before. And as in any explosion the impact makes concentric circles of an infinite number out into the world. Everything changed. I went home and broke up a relationship. I was dying. I had been dying for a long time.

I walked back through the house we had made together of hopes and dreams and as I gathered up my belongings to move out I made a ceremony for leaving. I went to every room and thanked it for the good times, for what I learned during the worst. I talked to the plants, smelled clothes, and touched the things that would no longer be intimate to me. It was not easy and I had to stop within the circle many times. I imagine when I die I will perform the same ceremony. My spirit, though anxious to leave the body of slow earth movement and pain, will turn briefly to acknowledge the husk it is leaving behind. Then it will go.

Protocol

Pikake is the jasmine flower.

Maile is a fragrant vine used to make leis for special occasions.

Tobacco is a sacred plant of the Mvskoke and for many other tribes. Plants have viability and purpose, just as anything created in this universe. There's a story told of how the plant came to the Mvskoke. A young couple who had just been married lie down together on their way back to the young warrior's encampment to make their home. Later, when the young man passed by the place, as he was savoring sweet memories, he saw a pretty little plant growing there. He tended it and every time he passed he stopped and took care of it. When it matured he took some of the good-smelling leaves from the plant. At his campfire there one night he was told by the creating spirit to put the leaves into the fire. The leaves smelled even better. He took them back to the old men of the tribe and told them the story of the plant. One of the men crumbled some of the leaves then smoked them in a hollowed-out corncob. The aroma swirled around the encampment, gave a sweet smell. The people agreed that the leaves were good and have used them ever since.

The Creeks valued the tobacco plant so highly they made it a warrior and gave it the war name *hitci*.

The tobacco cultivated by the Mvskoke was not the tobacco known today, rather of the *Nicotiana rustica,* a plant native to the central Andes (from *Southern Indians Myths and Legends,* compiled and edited by Virginia Pounds Brown and Laurella Owens, Beechwood Books, Leeds, Alabama, 1985, p. 68).

Morning Song

Since the first published edition of *A Map to the Next World,* this poem has become a song with repeated phrases to accommodate melody.

NEW POEMS, 1999–2001

In Praise of Earth

This poem was written as a commission from the Racine Chorus, in collaboration with Brent Michael Davids, the Mohegan composer and musician. The performed commission was titled, "She Is One of Us." It was first performed in October 2000.

Stickball is a game played among the Mvskoke with lacrosse-like sticks and a ball. It is called the "little brother of war" because it is meant to replace all-out war and was often used for resolution of disputes in Mvskoke communities.

Earth and *Sun* are capitalized as they are entities with spirit and soul and are known by many proper names.

Letter (with songline) to the Breathmaker

Hesaketvmese or *Maker of Breath* represents the wind spirit. Jean Hill Chaudhauri and Joyotpaul Chaudhauri, in their book *A Sacred Path, the Way of the Muscogee Creeks* (UCLA Indian Studies Center, 2001), make the point that the Christians turned Hesaketvmese into the Christian God, when he was just an assistant to Ibofanga, the ultimate and singular universal spirit.

Plumeria is also known by the name of frangipani. It is a fragrant flowering tree in Hawai'i that is often used in the making of leis. The name *frangipani* comes from Muzio Frangipani, a sixteenth-century Italian marquis. While living in Paris he created a perfume for scenting gloves based on bitter almonds, which is similar to the smell of red jasmine flowers (www.burkesbackyard.com.au/facts/2000/hawaii_36.html).

At the beginning of the season of the 2000 elections, the Washington State Republican Party overwhelmingly passed a resolution to terminate Indian tribal governments. This resolution called for the government to "immediately take whatever steps necessary to terminate all non-republican forms of government on Indian reservations." This extremist resolution was headed by the sponsor, John Fleming, a Skagit County delegate and non-Indian resident of an Indian reservation. He adamantly insisted that if American Indians resist, "the U.S. Army and the Air Force and the Marines and the National Guard are going to have to battle back."

This poem was an experiment to include this racist and hateful event in a poem, to see what would happen. Could the poem contain it? Destroy the poison? The first drafts name the Republican Party and the resolution. Eventually the direct references fell away. And history went on. The resolution did not become a plank in the national Republican Party but the hatefulness that wrote the resolution still chokes. Andrew Jackson is still here, as is Hernando de Soto, Cotton Mather, and all the rest of those who believe in the superiority of one people over another, one set of gods over another.

There is communication between planets, stars, and other heavenly bodies. All is alive, near and far, and we communicate by light, by senses, by all of the layers beyond the senses.

I Am Not Ready to Die Yet

Poi is a staple of the Hawaiian diet. It is made by pounding the taro root and is unique to the Hawaiian people.

Naming

Vanessa, Toshi and Tamarin Chee, and Krista Chico are granddaughters who are part of the Tvlvhasse Ceremonial grounds and take part in the women's ribbon dance. This is a children's poem.

Equinox

This poem is for Gregory Sarris.

Ah, Ah

Outrigger canoe paddling is a racing tradition of the Polynesians. I paddled the 2000 outrigger canoe season for Anuenue Canoe Club, the renowned Nappy Napoleon's club in Waikiki, Hawai'i. I began the paddling season of 2001 with the Marina Del Rey Canoe Club in southern California but traveling kept me away from too many practices and I had to reluctantly drop out from what is an excellent canoe club. There are outrigger racing clubs all over the Pacific and the North American Pacific coast. There is now even an outrigger canoe club in Italy.

Morning Prayers

The phrase *Carry us all to the top of the mountain* is derived from the Dr. Martin Luther King speech, "I've Been to the Mountaintop," delivered in support of the striking sanitation workers at Mason Temple in Memphis, Tennessee, on April 3, 1968, the day before he was assissinated.

The Everlasting

Ingrid Washinawatok was shot to death along with Terence Freitas and Lahena'e Gay near the Columbia/Venezuelan border after they were kidnapped on February 25, 1999. They were in the country at the request of the U'wa people of Columbia who have been fighting the Occidental Petroleum Company's plans to drill oil on ancestral U'wa lands.

The U'wa people issued a statement August 10, 1988, that said: "Today we feel that we're fighting a large and strong spirit that wants to beat us or force us to submit to a law contrary to that which Sira (God) established and wrote in our hearts, even before there was the sun and the moon. When faced with such a thing, we are left with no alternative than to continue fighting on the side of the sky and earth and spirits or else disappear when the irrationality of the invader violates the most sacred of our laws."

And If I Awaken in Los Angeles

The voice of jazz singer *Billie Holiday* carries centuries of grief. Her phrasing was impeccable, a balance between chains and flight.

It's Raining in Honolulu

The *second overthrow* refers to the *Cayetano* v. *Rice* decision in which the U.S. Supreme Court struck down Hawai'i's practice of allowing only the beneficiaries of the Office of Hawaiian Affairs (OHA), indigenous Hawaiians, to vote for OHA trustees.

OHA is a semi-autonomous trust designated to function as the primary agency for the betterment of the Native Hawaiian people and was created by popular vote of all Hawai'i's citizens.

Rushing the Pali

Pali means cliff in Hawaiian. The Pali is the name of the cliff over which Kamehameha's warriors pushed the O'ahu warriors in order to take over O'ahu and unite the islands by violence. It was pivotal battle in uniting the islands. The Pali is also the name of the highway that runs from H-1 in Honolulu over the Ko'olau's toward Kailua.

Kewalo is the name of a basin and surfing area on the south shore of O'ahu. Outcasts intended for sacrifice were once drowned here (*Place Names of Hawaii*, Pukui and Elbert and Mookini, University of Hawaii Press, 1974).

All acts of kindness are lights in the war for justice.